INSIDE

DISCOVERING BARCELONA'S CLASSIC INTERIORS

JOSEP M.BOTEY

PHOTOGRAPHS BY
PETER APRAHAMIAN

BARCELONA

**To my brother Silveri
and of course to Mireia.**

Phaidon Press Limited
140 Kensington Church Street,
London W8 4BN

First published 1992
© Phaidon Press Limited 1992

A CIP catalogue record of this book is
available from the British Library

ISBN 0 7148 2718 5

Printed in Singapore

Designed by
Stafford Cliff

Page 1: Palau Güell
Page 2: Casa Batlló
Page 6: Museu d'Art de Catalunya
Page 126: Col.legi de les Teresianes

INSIDE

BARCELONA

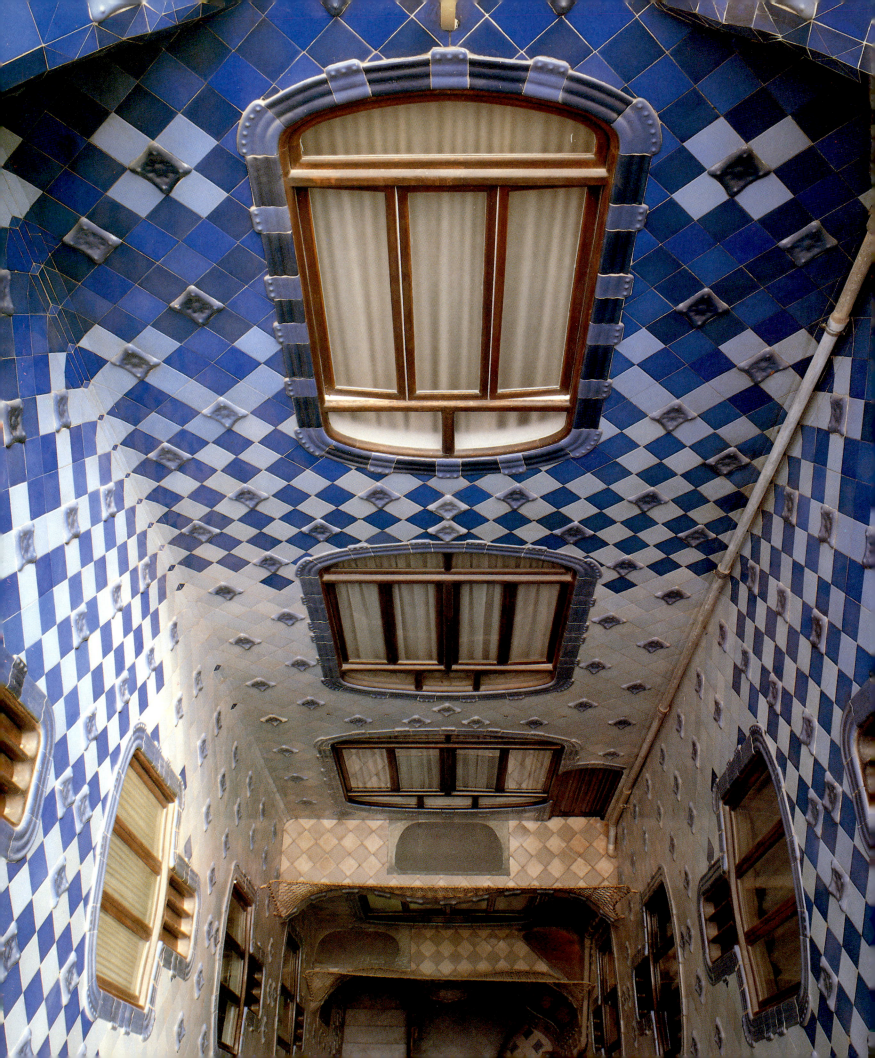

CONTENTS

INTRODUCTION 7

SHOPS 17

CLUBS & INSTITUTIONS 27

THEATRES, CINEMAS & MUSIC HALLS 35

BANKS, OFFICES & STATIONS 43

SCHOOLS & COLLEGES 49

HOTELS & HOSTELS 55

BARS & RESTAURANTS 61

LIBRARIÈS & ARCHIVES 71

GOVERNMENT & CIVIC BUILDINGS 77

HOSPITALS & RESIDENCES 95

MUSEUMS 99

PRIVATE HOUSES 109

ACKNOWLEDGEMENTS & BIBLIOGRAPHY 118

GAZETTEER 119

INDEX 127

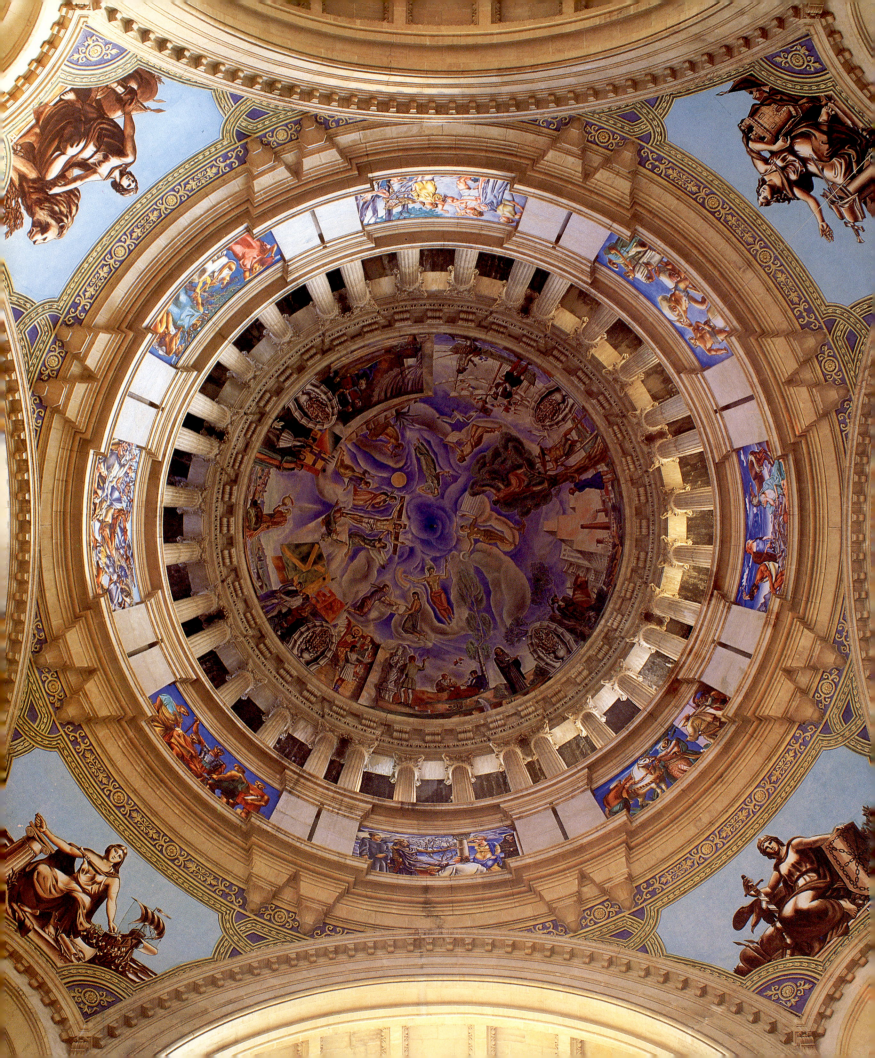

INTRODUCTION

I remember it perfectly because it happened to me some years ago in the old part of the city. At the time I was studying architecture and had planned to take some student friends from New York on a brief tour of Barcelona. We didn't have a lot of time that day, but before showing them the famous Casa Batlló by Gaudí I thought we should go to the old Academy of Medicine and Surgery which Ventura Rodríguez had built from a sketch by Blondel. It was late and we were in a bit of a hurry so, trying to find a parking space wherever I could, I turned left suddenly, something I hadn't meant to do. What had happened? Didn't I know where I was going? To save time, I asked directions, in Catalan of course, from the first person I saw.

'Sorry, I can't understand,' he said in English.

Amused by the situation, I explained what we were looking for. With no hesitation, the Englishman replied: 'Just go straight on. It's a few hundred metres ahead.'

In a flash I understood that I didn't really know Barcelona, that I lived in the city as if at a distance, in the lecture theatres of the University, with a feeling of possession which bordered on indifference, that same kind of indifference that is sometimes reflected in our eyes when we stare blankly at the same old corners of the family home. A foreigner, on the other hand, seemed to know the city well. He had probably made it his own because he was far away from his own country; perhaps he felt the need to love it with real passion, while I was still trapped by that sense of ownership which the classroom sometimes instils. I had yet to develop an in-depth vision of my city.

Since then I have informally related this anecdote many times to point out something which seems worth mentioning: we sometimes know other cities better than the one we were born in and which we call our own.

But is this really the case? Do we consciously adopt a city or does it somehow almost magically capture us? This is not an easy question to answer. We might imagine that the small circle which begins in us and extends to the maze of streets like a ripple on water would come back to us in equal measure. Or we might say that the entire city generates an energy with which we are each uniquely charged. Unlikely as it might seem, the city we live in slowly helps to mould our character, defining us - as Londoner, Parisian, Barcelonian - and comes to dictate the behaviour of its inhabitants. Shakespeare said that a city is its people; perhaps we should go one step further and turn this theory on its head to explore its opposite for just a moment. Could an apparent loss of reason be the stuff of the twentieth century? Is it possible that the habitats we have created will end up confusing us?

I am afraid that tomorrow's students of twentieth-century architecture will ask themselves a very similar question, for Barcelona is a city marked by this century.

As the architect A. de Moragas i Gallissà wrote, 'In the two thousand years of its history, the city of Barcelona has kept, in each period, an architecture with constant characteristics, as if the influences which came from abroad, when incorporated in this Mediterranean space, took on the nature of the city. Austerity, simplicity, severity and hope are repeated qualities. Sometimes not even poverty prevents discovery of the spirit of a town which has had to fight alone against its adversaries; a city which today must admit to a total lack of great monuments, especially from the fifteenth century.'

His evaluation is correct. From a historical point of view, Barcelona has characteristics similar to other large cities such as Marseilles, Genoa, Milan, Liverpool, Hamburg and Rotterdam, whose identity derives from being 'alternative', i.e. from their not being the political centre of a nation. Most of them are industrial ports, just the opposite of capitals like Vienna, Rome and Paris where the sea is far enough away for them to avoid the easy flow of a human tide. A port city is always, to some extent, a gateway. And it is this great entrance which can take in all that comes with time. It is the living, breathing present, built in the ante-room of the future.

The people of ancient Carthage knew this. It is to Carthage that Barcelona owes its name and the legendary history of its foundation. The Romans also knew it and took advantage of the coast to anchor their ships, as they extended the limits of the Mediterranean further to the west. It was Rome that gave Barcelona its character as a city: a structured hamlet which would continue growing right up to the present. Even today, the Roman Via Augusta is one of the city's most stately and prestigious avenues. Nor is it just a coincidence that the remains of the Roman presence should crop up so regularly. Roman Barcelona maintains an essentially subterranean life, but now and again, as in Fellini's unforgettable sketch in the film *Roma,* the construction work on a new underground station is stopped short due to the miraculous discovery of a Roman wall or the ochre- and blue-tinted mosaic pavement of a villa. It is in such moments, when time seems to stand still as the past is rediscovered, that the present loses its place in the foreground of life. And it is then that the people of Barcelona suddenly become aware of the value of their origins.

The Roman city was the foundation on which medieval Barcelona rose to its full splendour in the fifteenth century: a city which was built slowly and which closed itself off from the sea behind walls and fortifications, the sea that was at once the livelihood and an extension of the city. The narrow streets, ever darker and more winding, bewitched the Cabbalists of Gerona, Barcelona's neighbour to the north which at that time sheltered one of the most active Jewish communities in Europe. These same Jews set up new retreats in Barcelona for their rituals, vaulted chambers in which decision-making conclaves were held, entry to which was gained by skirting the city wall or by slipping through the inevitable secret passage at nightfall. Even today, in a quiet stroll through the formidable Gothic Quarter, we can discover the old Hebrew nomenclature and some stone signs which, at the time, were true guiding lights for the initiated.

It is perhaps from this period that the legend sprang that Barcelona lived with its back to the coast. But this was not always the case. Without a doubt, Barcelona's most important identifying characteristic is its being a port and for centuries the city lived from fishing and trade with the Mediterranean and the Middle East. The years just before the Renaissance were fruitful. The port was an important one and many ships left its docks to sail as far as Byzantium or to remain for more than a century in immortal Greece where Barcelona established a consulate in the fifteenth century.

The decline began during the reign of Fernando and Isabel. Their epic undertaking, or so-called 'Discovery', displaced the focus of interest from Europe to the west, and as a result trade with the eastern Mediterranean lost much of its impetus. Like Venice, Barcelona was left to flounder in stagnant waters. However, it was not this change of focus alone which relegated it to the background. Royal edicts excluded the Catalan people from participating in the colonization of America. Thus, while some European cities were living a truly golden age, Barcelona was left to look elsewhere, closed in on itself, wistfully standing by while the future knocked at other people's doors.

This dark period lasted for several hundred years. Barcelona's Renaissance was a washed-out version of the splendour of the Middle Ages. Forced to fight wars of independence and succession as a result of interests not its own, Barcelona never acquired a Baroque physiognomy, which if it had would undoubtedly have been a reflection of the city's own very particular quality.

Towards the end of the eighteenth century and all through the nineteenth, however, a rebirth was under way in the city. Liberal ideas from France, an economic resurgence and progressive industrialization made Barcelona the mercantile centre of the country. Likewise, the Catalan people who, until that time, had visited America only as civil servants of the Crown, gained the right to free trade with the American colonies. Good at business, they did not waste the opportunity so often denied them before to make their fortunes overseas. Those fortunes made by businessmen and adventurers meant a sudden injection of capital into a country which had been living in the shadows for several centuries, crippled by a failing economy. In a short time the foundations of modern Barcelona were laid down. In 1859 the Cerdà plan was drawn up which would determine the current layout of the streets; the city was awarded the organization of the 1888 Universal Exhibition; but above all, thanks to a philanthropic upper middle class, the development of the arts was strongly promoted.

Thus began the *Renaixença,* a true linguistic and plastic rebirth which would make its mark on this rich turn-of-the-century period. It was during this time that Barcelona became the capital of *Modernisme,* an expression peculiar to Catalonia denoting Art Nouveau and *Jugendstil.* The works of Gaudí, Puig i Cadafalch and Domènech i Montaner are magnificent examples of a movement which, though cities such as Vienna, Paris and Glasgow boast notable examples, is forever linked to Barcelona's urban landscape.

This resurgence was intense and complete: neo-Gothic constructions, buildings which look like castles or fabulous caverns, always furnished and decorated with eye-catching stained glass, floral motifs and dream-like women; all the exuberant medieval imagination which evoked the city's previous period of greatness and which still played against the backdrop of popular consciousness.

In this way, in line with one of the basic characteristics of Catalonia, a legion of anonymous craftsmen put their talent to the service of this great metropolitan undertaking. The fruit of this creative fervour was the development of a taste for allegory, zoomorphic scenes (iron dragons and golden butterflies) and oriental prints, which decorate the façades of some of the buildings that have been preserved.

The decline of the Spanish colonial empire began in 1898 and had negative repercussions on the society of Barcelona as well as other large Continental cities, making the beginning of the twentieth century difficult, violent and convulsive. Barcelona experienced popular uprisings which shattered its calm, and between 1914 and the Spanish Civil War the heart of the city was a great sounding board for the principal events in Europe. Austro-Hungarian nobles arrived here, fugitives from a dying empire, as did prominent artists such as Schoenberg, who finished one of his most important works, *Moses and Aaron,* in Barcelona. There were harsh confrontations between the working class and the industrial leaders, yet the city embarked once again on what could be called one of its cyclical projects to foster its own image as a city fit to take its place in the international community: the organization of the 1929 International Exhibition, which produced some gems of modern architecture, such as the German Pavilion by the young Mies van der Rohe.

With the proclamation of the Second Republic in 1931, Catalonia recovered laws and civil liberties and became a centre for important anarchistic movements. Aware of its social responsibilities, the Mancomunitat de Catalunya (the regional Catalan government) built schools, hospitals and recreation centres for the lower classes. The winds of change touched the streets of the city in this way until the outbreak of the Civil War in 1936. Then Barcelona opened its arms to all who would defend freedom. This was the time of André Malraux, Claude Simon, George Orwell, Ernest Hemingway and others, and of a wave of fervent international brigadiers. It was a unique period in the history of this century for, besides fighting fascism, it witnessed the first open confrontation between communism and anarchism. Beneath this combative and enthusiastic Barcelona, lay another which was hidden and turbulent, a dirty and decadent city which would inspire the writings of Jean Genet and Pierre de Mandiargues: the Barcelona of the red-light district. The city, better known internationally than any other as a literary focal point, was mortally wounded by the fascist triumph. A new, difficult and dark period began, which lasted several decades and included imperialistic policies reminiscent of the time of Fernando and Isabel. But eternal Barcelona, ever renewable, survived this latest humiliation and, thanks to the awakening of democracy in the 1970s, is now living in a state of grace which has made possible the hosting of the 1992 Olympic Games.

My purpose in recalling the past is to put the city in context. Many famous buildings no longer exist; others have been transformed. The city has suffered almost cyclical variations in its fortunes. When Catalonia disappeared as a country there was a dark period when Barcelona lost its way. Its architectural inheritance has been considerably reduced. However, there have been survivals from two great architectural periods which colour the most memorable aspects of the city: the Gothic with its sense of justice which belongs to a time of splendour when Catalonia was broadening its horizons throughout the Mediterranean; and the exuberant flourishing of *Modernisme* in the nineteenth century. The *modernista* movement is still alive, though transformed by rationalism which has altered that fluid quality emanating from a period of rebirth, consolidation and political hopefulness in the world of urban planning and design.

However, old Barcelona will live on into the next millennium and it is good to be able to say that the city itself has decided (although at times that decision was made for it) how to use its wealth as an almost daily event. The chemist's shop, for example, is still a chemist's shop; the bakery, a bakery; the herbalist's shop a herbalist's shop. This might look like a way of spending the city's assets, but it also means that the past finds expression in a spirit which, according to Josep Pla, is 'inseparable from freedom, democracy and, in general, everything connected to modern life'.

We must not forget that Barcelona has never had much space to expand outwards. Medieval walls succeeded the Roman and only once was there a single splendid opportunity for growth: Idelfons Cerdà's *Eixample*. Over the centuries Barcelona has absorbed the villages which surrounded it (Sants, Horta and Sarrià) creating peripheral neighbourhoods with individual personalities. In the 1960s, strong waves of immigration resulted in the consolidation of the areas surrounding turn-of-the-century Barcelona into a greater metropolis. Its geographic setting (sea and mountain have always limited territorial expansion) gave rise to this urgency to expand inward, to transform whole neighbourhoods in the heart of the city or to give new life to run-down buildings, restoring them for new uses. For example, the Royal Shipyards are being used to house the Maritime Museum and the Picasso Museum is housed in the one of the old palaces on Carrer Montcada. Along other lines, the Pia Almoina uses contemporary ideas to transform architectural styles of the past, and has found a creative way to bridge the intervening years.

Clearly the criteria used in making choices from a world as complex as the modern Barcelona I have described are both subjective and objective. We need parameters to explain not only how the choices were made, but also to provide keys to help overall understanding. The philosophy of this book is not to offer a new guide to the city, but rather to attempt to immerse itself in the city without preconceptions and to offer a unique, intimate look from the inside. Obviously, it is likely to be incomplete, but the original idea was to approach the task with only one hundred images: one hundred sometimes fragile expressions which yet remain true to the original undertaking. I believe that this book, unlike those based on the more monumental cities, Paris and London, must be approached from a different perspective, for one thing because Barcelona forms an indivisible part of Catalonia and the Catalans are an essentially insular people. For this reason, I did not want to concentrate on those architectural styles which already enjoy widespread commentary, but on unusual interiors which are difficult to get at; because once the Catalans have been persuaded to open up, their generosity is immediately visible in these interiors.

The difficulty in making a choice among private houses has been due to the shortage of original interiors and their owners' wish to maintain their privacy. But once inside, the architecture, interior decoration and individual touches are seen to epitomize the way of life of the people of Barcelona. So in seeking to describe these private houses - so lived in and inviting - I have chosen a summer home which has undergone a process of transformation: Casa Callejo-Amat in the Collserola woods. This is a particularly quiet spot which, at least in the early years of this century, was well away from the city centre. Such settings evoke the atmosphere of perpetual summer of the bourgeoisie, where the sun was always filtered through large and shady trees.

Other buildings have kept their original furniture and decoration, taking advantage of the marvellous atmosphere around which the space was initially planned, while in the offices of the Casa Batlló, or the Convention Bureau in the Casa Lleó i Morera the original elements have been preserved to fit in with activities more in keeping with today's pace of life.

Barcelona is rich in public buildings which, though decoratively varied, have continued to function without conflicting with the explicit purposes for which they were created. These are places which are at once spiritually austere and full of vitality. Such is the case of the Palau de la Generalitat (fourteenth to seventeenth centuries), headquarters of the government of Catalonia; alterations did not stop it being the finest example of Renaissance architecture in the city. The same is true of the palatial Govern Civil building (eighteenth century), the Tinell (fifteenth century) or the Llotja de Mar (sixteenth to seventeenth century), surprising and unforgettable heart of the city's stock market. Jealously preserved, this inheritance enjoys an active and permanent life which has become absolutely necessary for the civic health of the community.

Irreparable damage has been done to Barcelona's shops, centres of intense commercial activity which have been virtually destroyed by successive drastic alterations. This does not, however, stop the oldest from proudly displaying their treasures, warts and all, despite the passage of the years. Finding completely intact *modernista* pharmacies, bakeries and patisseries, or even older places, such as the Subira candle-maker's, showpieces of another time, happily transports us back into the past.

Conversions of old, grand and beautiful buildings which were originally planned as private houses in the *Eixample* and which have recently been transformed into spectacular commercial spaces, such as Vinçon, deserve separate mention; the same is true of other parts of strictly family dwellings, used for commercial or industrial purposes, which have now been converted into shops such as B.D. (Barcelona Design) or Loewe, external ornamental motifs being destroyed in the latter case.

In general, banks provide further proof of an interest in adapting to a new era without overlooking previous periods; most make an effort to get back the atmosphere of historic buildings, a good example being the offices of the Banca Catalana in the Rambla, or the Centre Cultural de la Fundació la Caixa. The first is a clear case of a turn-of-the-century office interior where the woodwork and somewhat archaic layout are still intact, revealing a clear intention on the part of the bank to bear witness to Barcelona's economic and commercial splendour. The second, in the Palau Macaya, represents the acquisition of a space for cultural use which retains, as far as possible, the atmosphere of the past.

It was not by chance, then, that these past times inspired a movie by Antonioni *(The Reporter)* or one of Losey's later films.

It is precisely in recognition of these times gone by and in the belief that Barcelona will continue to be at the forefront in times to come that I have accepted the gratifying task of opening my city to you: this well-known, yet mysterious lady for whom, as an architect, I experience true passion every day.

CHRONOLOGY

1ST CENTURY BC

Founding of the Roman colony Iulia Augusta Paterna Faventia Barcino.

5TH CENTURY AD

Ataulf makes Barcelona the capital of the Visigoth kingdom (415).

8TH CENTURY

Muslim invasion (716-19).

9TH CENTURY

Beginning of the Reconquest. Stabilization of the Charlemagne monarchy in the principality in spite of the constant Muslim invasions (801).

10TH CENTURY

Barcelona becomes the backbone of an autonomous Catalan power. Al-Mansur occupies and plunders the town (985).

11TH CENTURY

Work begins on the new cathedral that will replace the ancient palaeo-Christian basilica, and on new parishes in new urban settlements around the town (1058).

12TH CENTURY

The Count of Barcelona consolidates his political power in the Mediterranean. With the birth of the middle class, maritime trade opens to the Mediterranean.

13TH CENTURY

Jaume I the Conqueror creates the Consell de Cent, main governmental body of the city (1262).

14TH CENTURY

Barcelona becomes one of the most important Mediterranean towns.
Social, political and economic crisis in the entire principality (high mortality rate between 1333 and 1348). Pinnacle of Gothic art.

15TH CENTURY

Instability. The aristocrats and the craftsmen struggle for political control of the Consell de Cent (Busca and Biga). Drop in Mediterranean trade. In 1412, because of the Compromís de Casp, or Caspe Treaty, the Castilian dynasty of Trastámara (Fernando and Isabel) takes over the government of the principality. Civil war, 1462-72. Barcelona becomes the seat of the Diputació General or Generalitat, and its influence is extended to cover other Catalan towns.

16TH CENTURY

Institutions are converted. Ferran II promotes the aristocracy to the Consell de Cent.
Revival of trade and artisan economy.
Growing activity in the shipyards, as well as in guild life. Foundation of new religious orders under the impetus of the Counter-Reformation.
Construction of the wharf and civil and religious buildings. The Renaissance influences architectural creation and promotes university studies.

17TH CENTURY

Economic recession (wool industry, Mediterranean trade and guild production) provokes social unrest and political fragmentation. In 1640 begins a

period of violent confrontation with France. Urban growth is halted although some Baroque-style religious buildings are constructed.
Barcelona's surrender to Felipe IV gives the city a military air.

18TH CENTURY

The War of the Spanish Succession of 1705 paralyses the city. Felipe V begins a new institutional policy of repression of the Catalan identity (abolition of the Consell de Cent). Period of free trade.
1757 Disappearance of the Castilian monopoly of the American colonial market with the participation of the Catalan textile industry. Significant commercial growth. Birth of the new working class.
Creation of numerous scientific, academic and technical institutions. Liberal intellectual life. Last manifestations of Baroque and first examples of Neo-classicism.

19TH CENTURY

Napoleonic rule from 1808 to 1814. Political instability and loss of great part of the colonial market. Beginning of the Industrial Revolution (cotton, wool, iron and steel).

1848 Inauguration of the first section of the Barcelona-Mataró railway.
1833 Barcelona, cultural capital of the *Renaixença,* or Catalan Renaissance, a movement of romantic origin which promotes Catalan nationalism (1892 Bases de Manresa), which is transformed in *Modernisme.*
1859 Need for urban restructuring: Cerdà's plan for the *Eixample* (Extension).
1868 Fall of absolute monarchy.
1873 First Spanish Republic. The workers' movement acquires extensive political power.
1888 Universal Exhibition.

20TH CENTURY

New industrialization impetus.
1874 to **1931** Bourbonic restoration.
1907 Creation of the Mancomunitat of Catalonia.
1909 Tragic Week. Barcelona, Spanish capital of unionized workers.
1910 *Noucentisme* replaces *Modernisme.*
1929 The International Exhibition in Barcelona allows for urban renovation despite the Wall Street crash and the critical situation between the wars.
1930 to **1939** Industrial and agricultural impoverishment of Spain. Urban immigration.

Barcelona assumes the role of political motor of Catalonia. Urban reinterpretation despite being a period of frustrated projects (Barcelona Olympic Games, etc.).
1936 to **1939** Spanish Civil War. Politicians, intellectuals and artists flee.
1939 to **1957** Barcelona becomes a metropolis. Appearance of suburbs around the city.
1960 New urban planning vision: Barcelona Municipal Charter (movement of factories, division of the city, construction of housing and large industrial estates). Reappearance of desire for higher international profile.
1973 to **1979** Political transition towards democracy. Urban consolidation.
1978 Spanish Constitution. Recovery of democracy.
1979 Demographic standstill and economic recession. Project to recover Barcelona's seafront.

Since Spain's entry into the EEC, Barcelona has become a city with its face turned towards Europe. It has established an economic policy based on technology and the tertiary sectors.
The 1992 Olympic Games have opened the way to an architecture that is both evocative and innovative and has an international flavour.

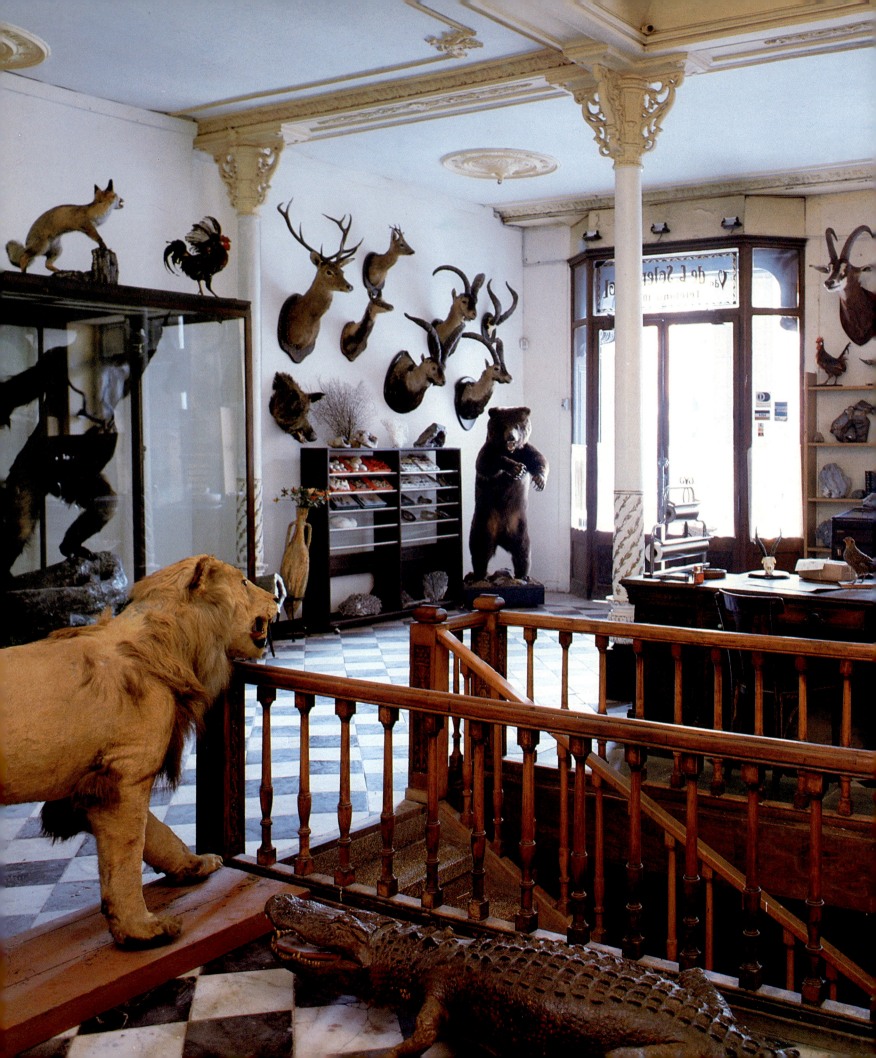

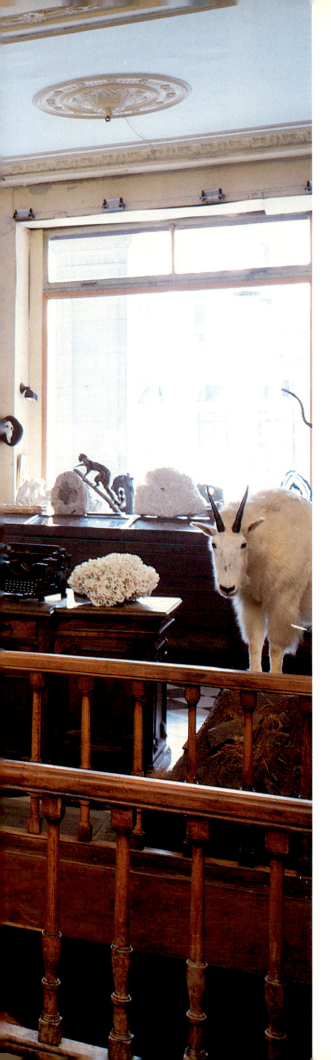

SHOPS

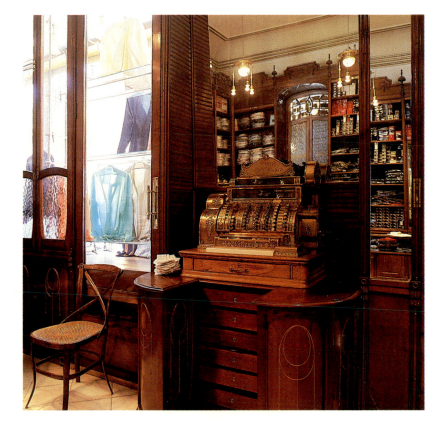

CASA PALAU

Like something out of a story by Stevenson or Poe, a visit to the Casa Palau can be a curious, not to say disturbing, experience. Founded in 1889, the taxidermist's premises were moved to the Plaça Reial in 1926. Skeletons were reconstructed in the basement, the taxidermist's workshop was located upstairs, and the ground floor housed the business itself. Palm trees in the courtyard give the impression of a strange painting of some kind of urban oasis.

Alfonso XIII entrusted this prestigious firm with his favourite horse's leg and Dalí, ever excessive, thought nothing of buying 200,000 ants and a rhinoceros. Whether or not the rhino horn's legendary powers were effective he was reluctant to disclose.

CAMISERIA XANCÓ

In the heart of the Rambla de les Flors, the interior of this shirtmaker's shop is virtually intact, as if mindless of the passage of time. The shirts, neatly arranged on hand-carved wooden shelves, change annually with the dictates of fashion, the faithful cash register ringing up with its own idiosyncratic note the changes in price as the decades flow by.

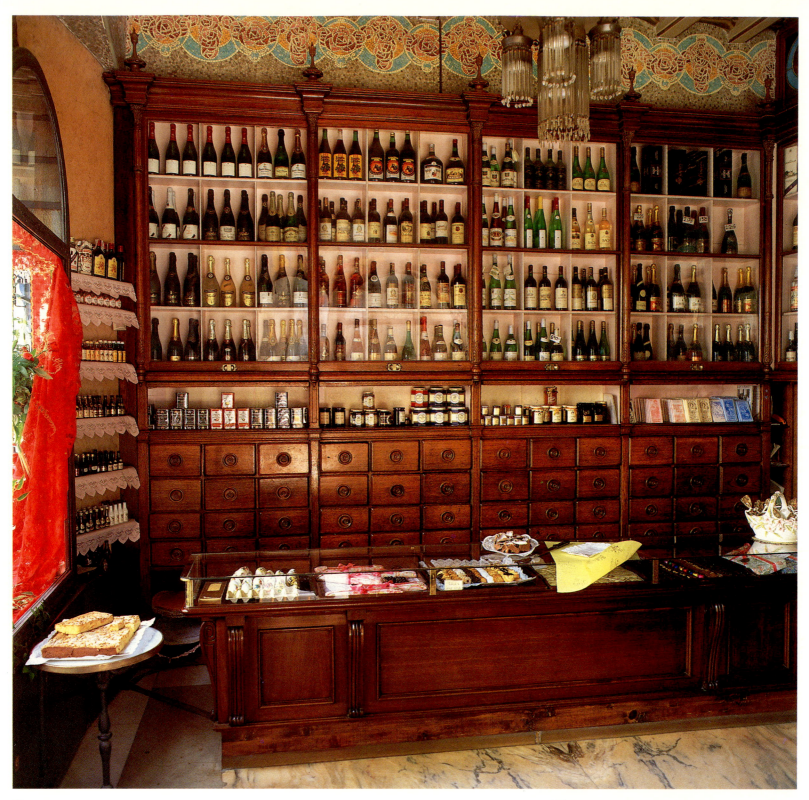

PASTISSERIA ESCRIBÀ

Modernity and tradition are paired in this ambitious piece of restoration started in 1986 by Christian Escribà, heir to a long line of distinguished Catalan pastrycooks. The façade of the old Casa Figueres on the Ramblas preserves the splendid modernista mosaic but the interior of the patisserie itself offers even greater pleasures. One of Barcelona's big attractions is finding paradises like this one where the sweet-toothed's every whim can be indulged.

FARMÀCIA MALLOL BALMAÑA

Progress has wrought inevitable transformations on the interiors of Barcelona's old chemist's shops, though some still remain. The Estrella, now called Mallol Balmaña, was owned by a well-known pharmacist in the mid nineteenth century. The style is reminiscent of the Fernandine epoch, together with the classical details in the seats and fluted pillars. The ornate ceramic jars date from 1920.

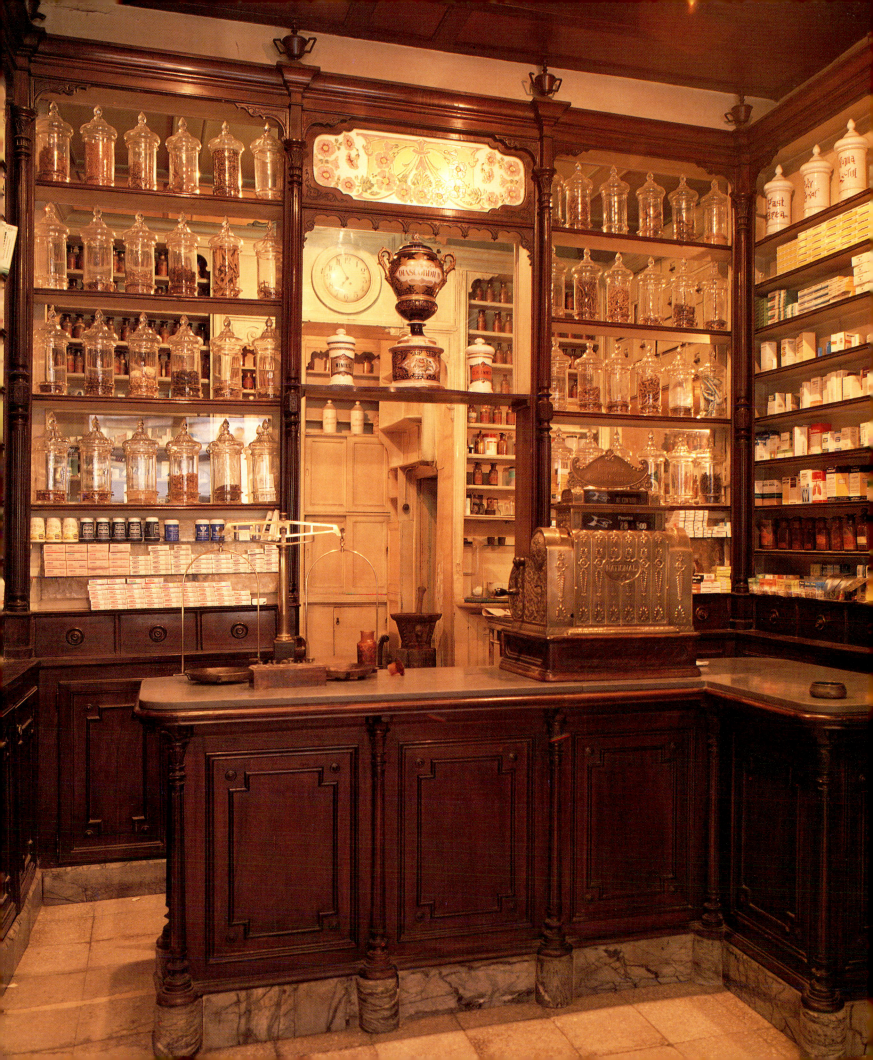

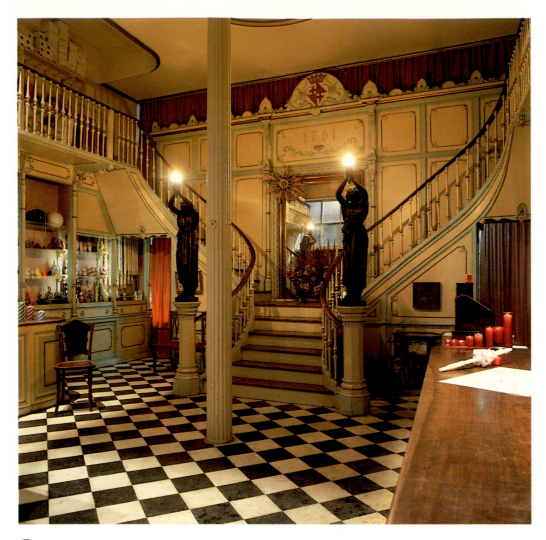

CERERIA SUBIRÀ

Like guardians of its elegant stairway these two magnificent candle-carrying polychrome plaster figures greeted this old shop's original customers who came in search of new clothes. The dress shop was built in 1847 but in 1909, on the opening of the Via Laietana, Barcelona's oldest surviving candlemaker's - founded in 1791 - moved here. The gilded woodwork adds to a sense of time immemorial. Attracted by the strange and antiquated atmosphere, Salvador Dalí was a frequent visitor.

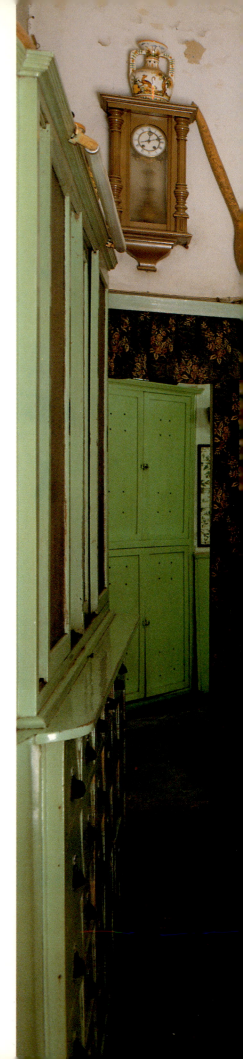

HERBORISTERIA ENORMES

In one of the oldest shops of its kind, in one of the city's oldest streets, you may find that special and long-searched-for herb concealed in one of these well-ordered drawers, each exuding its own very particular scent. The knowledgeable owner acts as herbalist, doctor, adviser and confidant to his many customers.

20

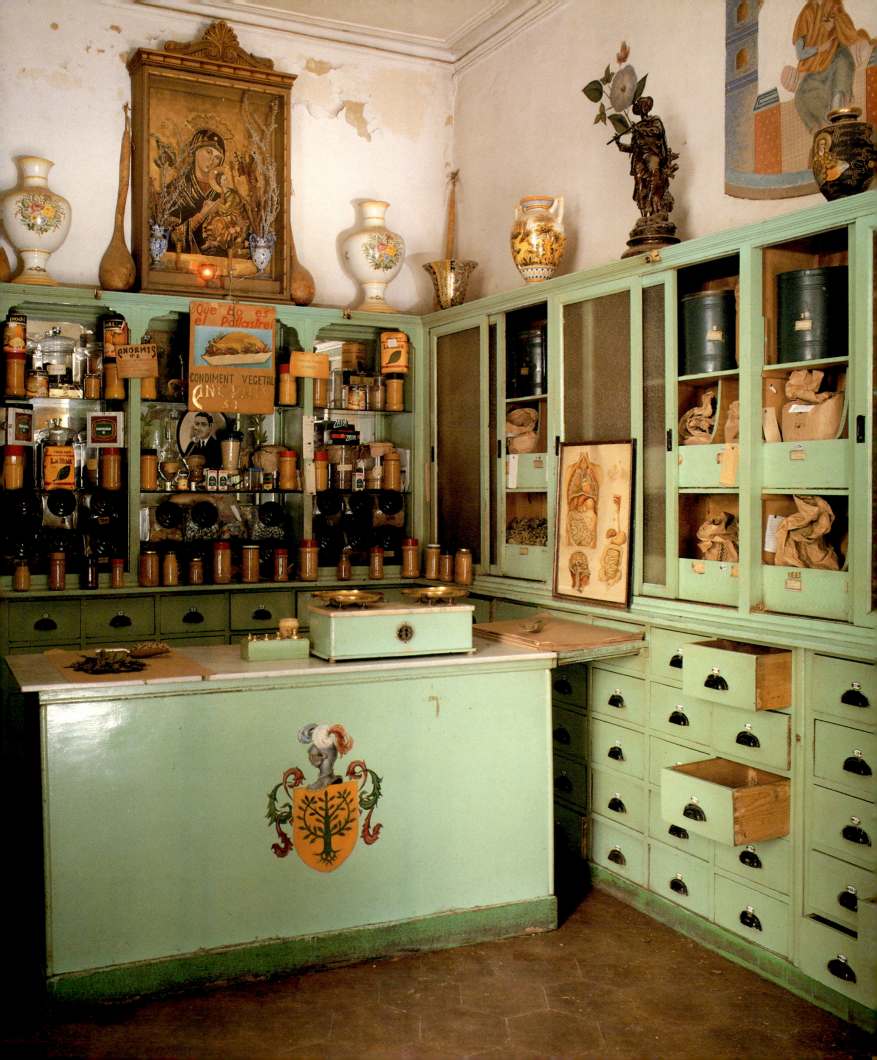

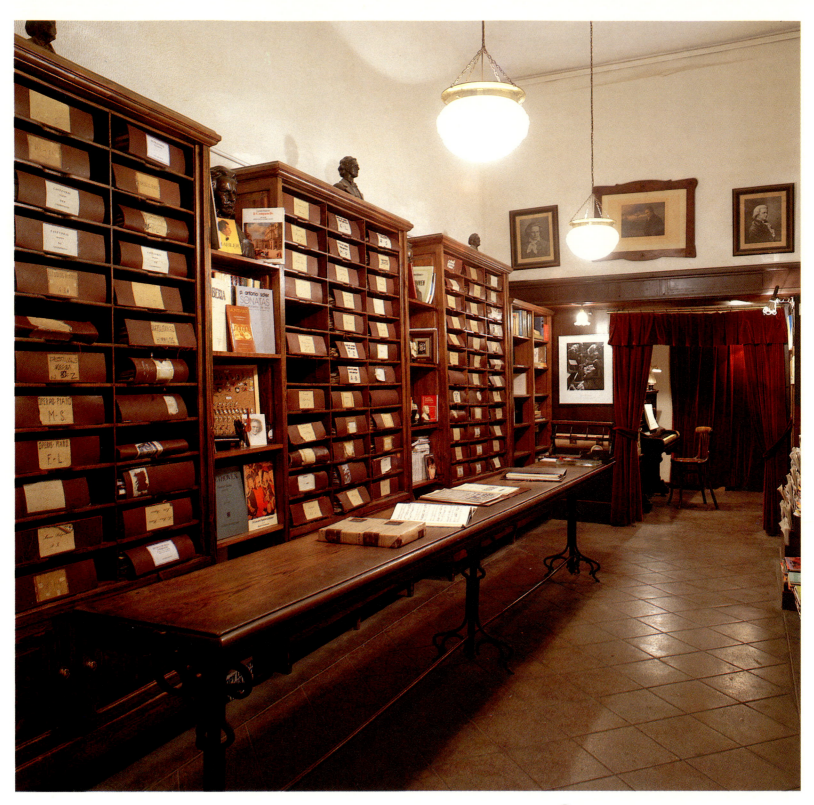

CASA BEETHOVEN

This music shop has been called Casa Beethoven since 1915 after the owner, a pianist, built up an important archive of music. Musicians from all over the world have come here since. Being so near the Liceu guarantees a constant liveliness in this intimate and inspirational setting. Above the quadrangluar floor plan, the panelled walls and wooden counters exude a resinous sweetness and create a warm and private space when the sun goes down.

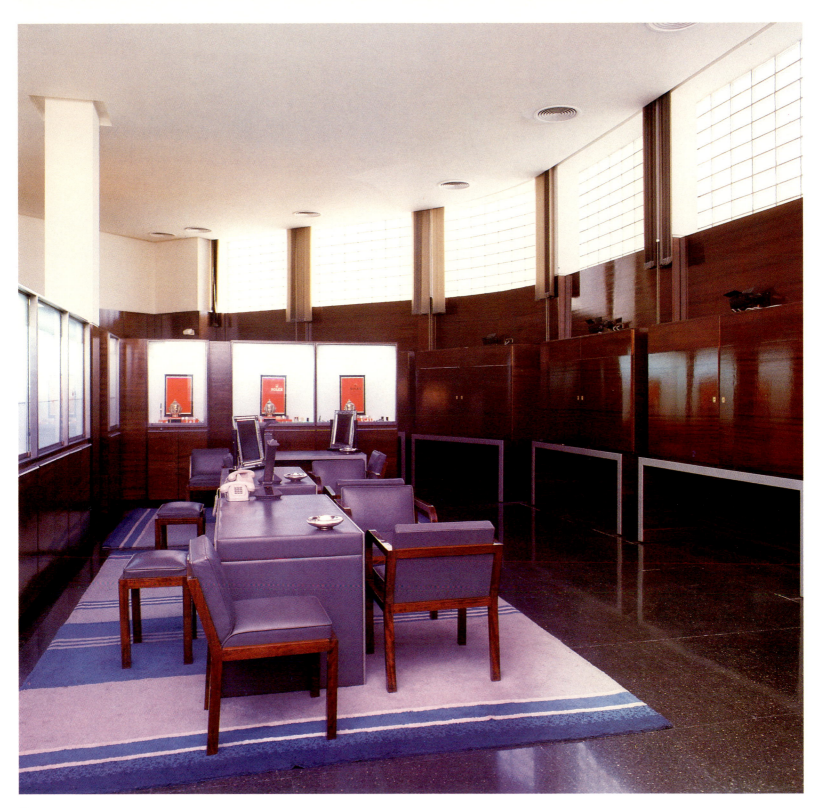

JOIERIA ROCA

A beautiful example of rationalism is to be seen in this interior of a jeweller's, the work of the architect Josep Lluis Sert. Yet in 1931 his work was greeted with hostility and controversy, breaking as it did with current bourgeois standards of 'good taste'. More than an architectural realization, what we have here is a complete concept: space, light, colour and furniture still in perfect condition and still surprisingly contemporary in feeling.

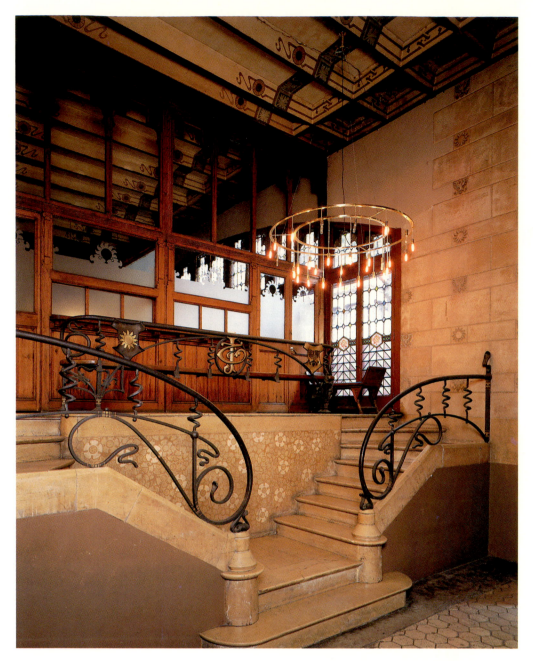

CASA THOMAS
(B.D. EDICIONS DE DISSENY)

Originally built by Domènech i Montaner at the end of the nineteenth-century, here are to be found the most prestigious international designs, everything from furniture by Gaudí, Alvar Aalto, Walter Gropius and Le Corbusier to carpets by Juan Gris. An exquisite shop, where container and contents have a common feeling for good design.

VINÇON

Under its novel appearance, Vinçon's demonstrates the endless possibilities of modern design. Its classical exterior, so typical of Barcelona's Eixample at the turn of the century, remained unaltered when the emporium opened in 1929 as a wholesale outlet for the sale of German porcelain; inside, the layout allows for a remarkable number of settings for a variety of products. In the open and accessible space the different wares mingle harmoniously under elegant and conducive lighting.

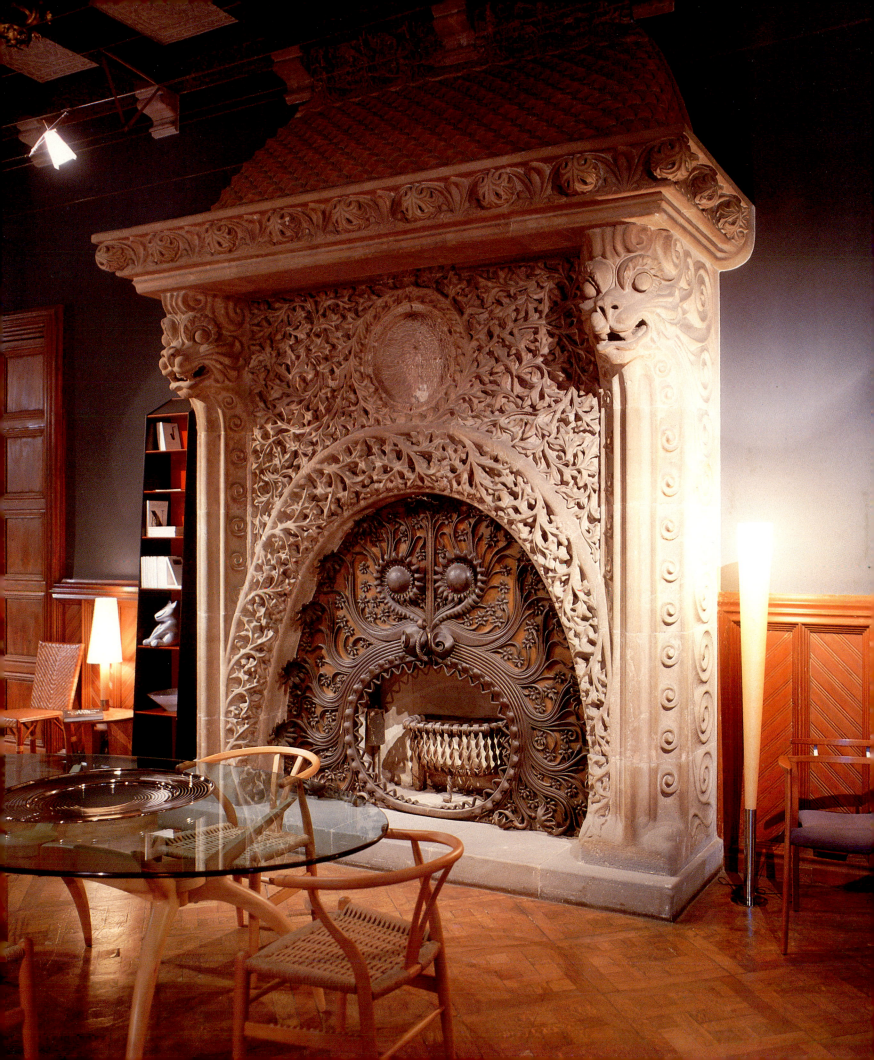

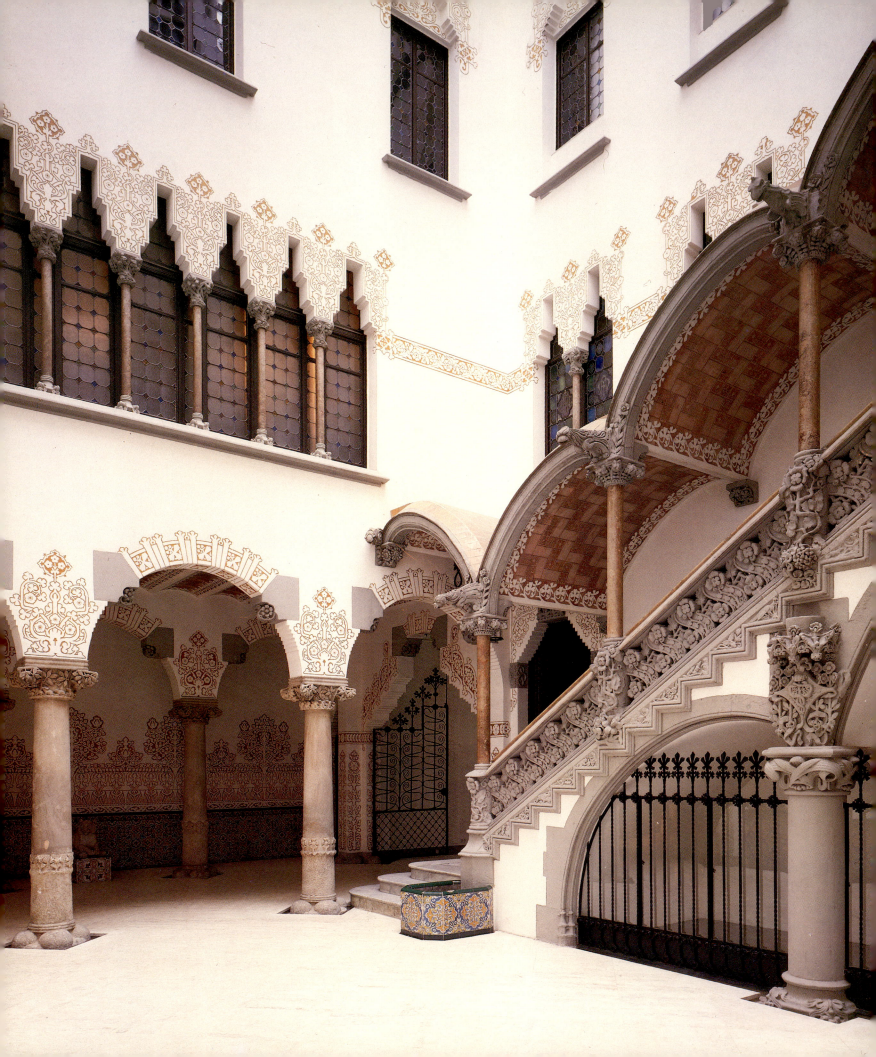

CLUBS & INSTITUTIONS

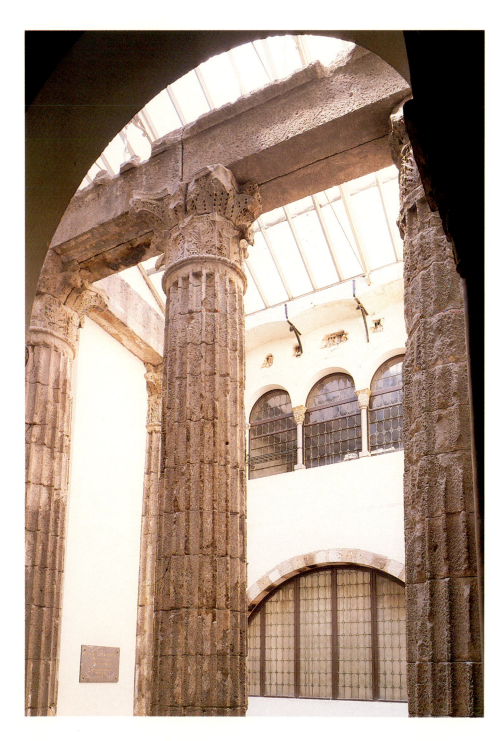

CENTRE CULTURAL DE LA FUNDACIÓ 'LA CAIXA'

The medieval courtyard in Barcelona was so important that it still existed when Modernisme *came into being and became the model for the superior Mediterranean house as here in the Palau Macaya designed in 1901 by Puig i Cadafalch and one of the finest examples from the architect's* modernista *period.*
The building was carefully selected by the Caixa de Pensions as its cultural centre and since its restoration has had a big attraction for artists and intellectuals.

CENTRE EXCURSIONISTA DE CATALUNYA

This splendid fourteenth-century building is one of the best examples of medieval civic architecture in private use in Barcelona.
Among other points of interest, such as the façade and the vestibule, are these amazing columns from the Roman temple of Augustus, salvaged during the remodelling of the interior courtyard in 1905. The sense of arrogance emanating from them at the heart of this Gothic building serves as an eternal reminder of the conqueror's triumph.

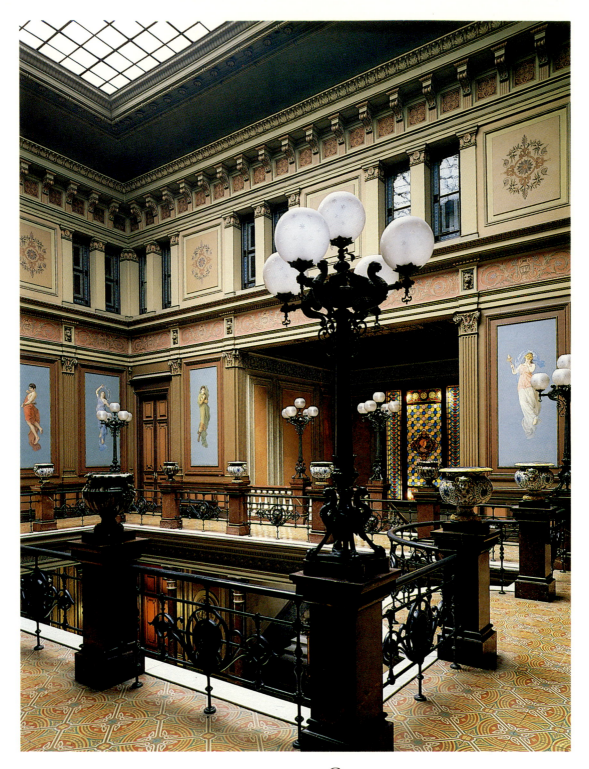

COLLEGI D'ADVOCATS

The original Palau Cassades, now the home of the Bar Association, has been partially preserved and faces on to Carrer Mallorca. The garden and what were once the stables have been given a new look. The palace courtyard, once with a fountain at its centre, is now covered by a large skylight through which light filters with an almost magical touch on to the multicoloured marble columns. A staircase with cast-iron and marble banister leads us up to the first floor, the stairwell finely decorated with delicately painted murals and ceramic tiles.

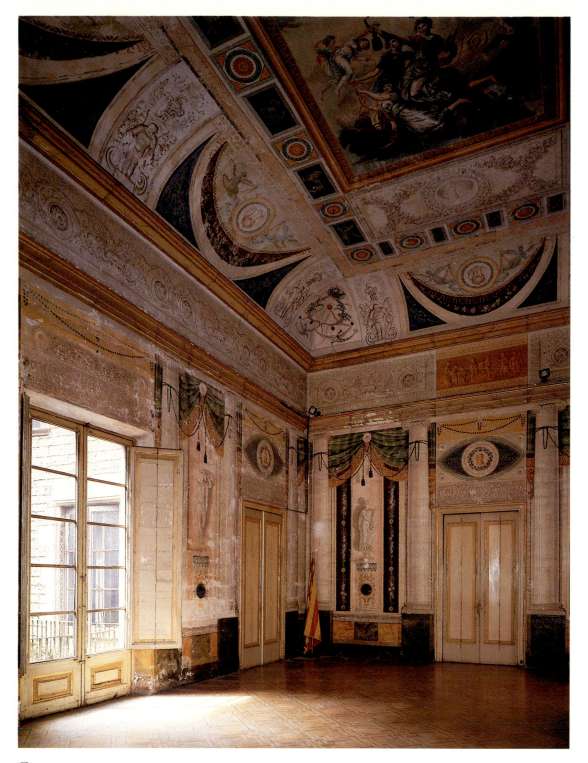

OMNIUM CULTURAL

The austere Palau Dalmases, with its bare
walls and sparse moulding, is a good example of
Catalan Baroque. Even the staircase in this
well-proportioned civic building, surmounted by
rampant arches on Solomonic columns with a
banister illustrating the abduction of Europa
and Neptune's chariot, though typically
Baroque, reflects the perfect orderliness of the
Catalan influence. Only the paintings on the
walls are more ornamentally exuberant and
closer to more traditional Baroque.

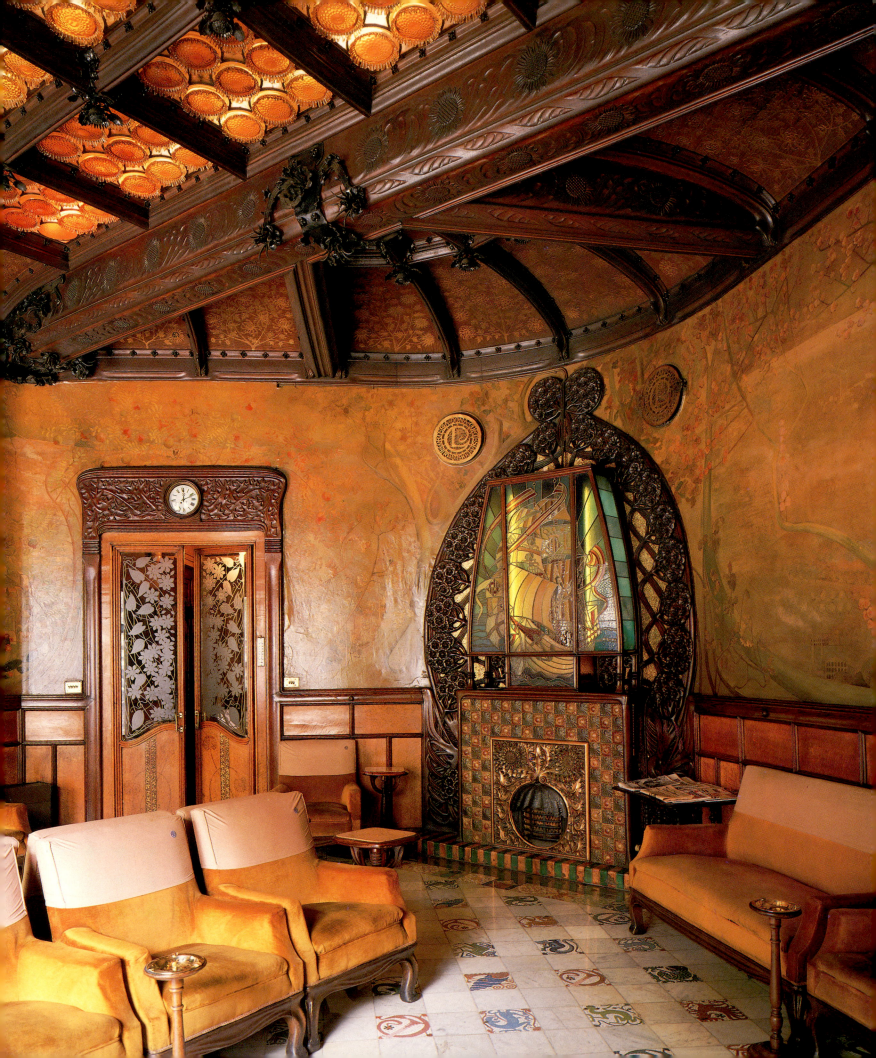

CERCLE DEL LICEU

After one of their unforgettable performances, Kraus, Carreras or Caballé come here to dine. This holy of holies for music lovers is a pleasant complement - for the club members - to the great opera galas. Built in 1847 during the reconstruction of the Gran Teatre del Liceu, the private rooms of the Cercle look out directly on to the crowded Ramblas. In keeping with the romantic spirit of the Catalan Renaixença, its members decorated the club with magnificent stained glass by A. Marti, furniture by the Busquets brothers, and the great chimney created by F. Vidal. No longer a private residence, it was one of the most exquisite at the time in Europe. Traditionally exclusively masculine, women are still today barred from certain areas, and in others are not allowed to sit down. When the club was residential, years ago, it was one of the most desirable places to stay in the city.

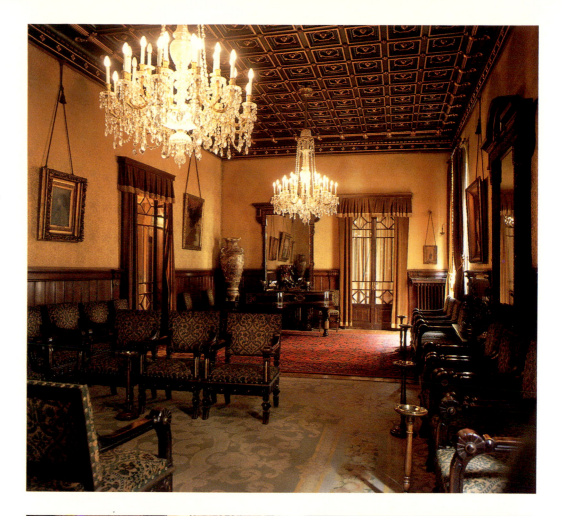

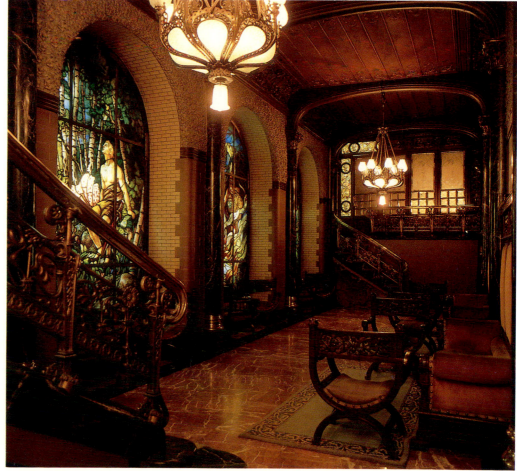

CERCLE EQÜESTRE

In the entrance hall to one of the jewels of Barcelona stands this great marble and carved-stone staircase. No one who visits the Cercle Eqüestre (also known as the Palau Samanillo) can fail to be captivated by its interiors. Works by Sorolla, Martí i Alsina and Clarà decorate the grand salons and are framed by fine polychrome plaster mouldings which set off and define each room. Intricately carved carouba wood decorates the archways.

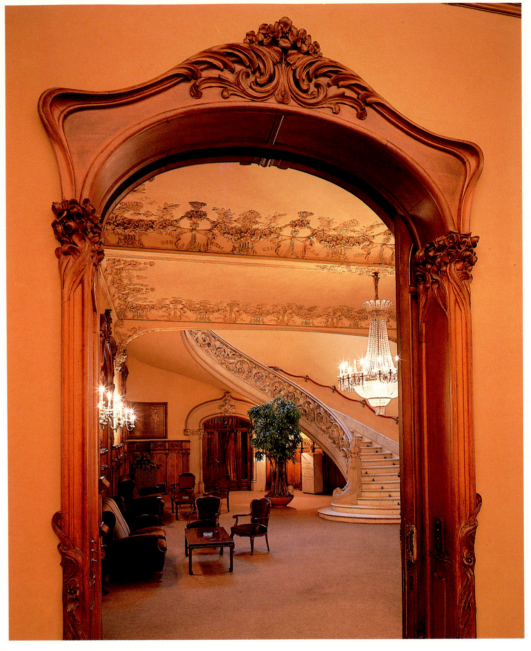

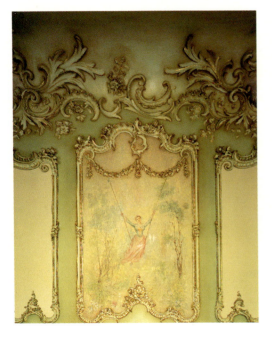

EDITORIAL ENCICLOPÈDIA CATALANA

As promoters of Catalan culture for many years now, this publishing house could not have found a better setting for its central offices than this house commissioned by Rupert Garriga i Molina in 1899 from the architect Enric Sagnier i Villavechia. Sagnier's work was greatly admired by the Catalan bourgeoisie because it agreed with traditional taste, had a French air and a touch of Modernisme, *yet was without Gaudí's discordance or Domènech i Montaner's intense commitment. The pictorial decoration of the walls and ceilings, oil paint applied directly to plaster, here seen in the girl on a swing, still expresses the building's essential spirit.*

REIAL ACADÈMIA DE MEDICINA I CIRURGIA

Pere Virgili, the King's surgeon, was commissioned by Carlos III to establish a college of surgery in Barcelona; between 1761 and 1764, Ventura Rodríguez was in charge of the construction of this unique building based on Neo-classical principles. Using the rotunda as a theme his functional system centres on the positioning of the bases which, arranged like terraced concentric rings, form an amphitheatre round the operating table. The impeccable geometric precision of the lines can be appreciated as much today as in the eighteenth century.

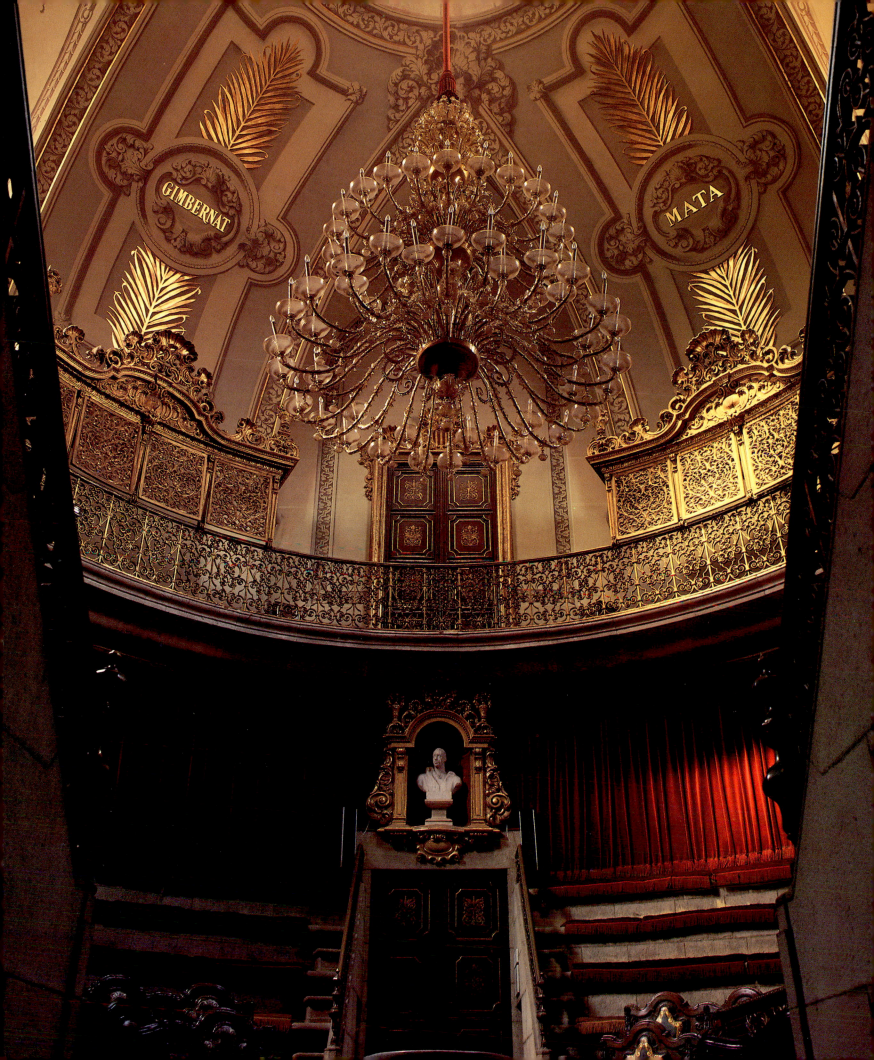

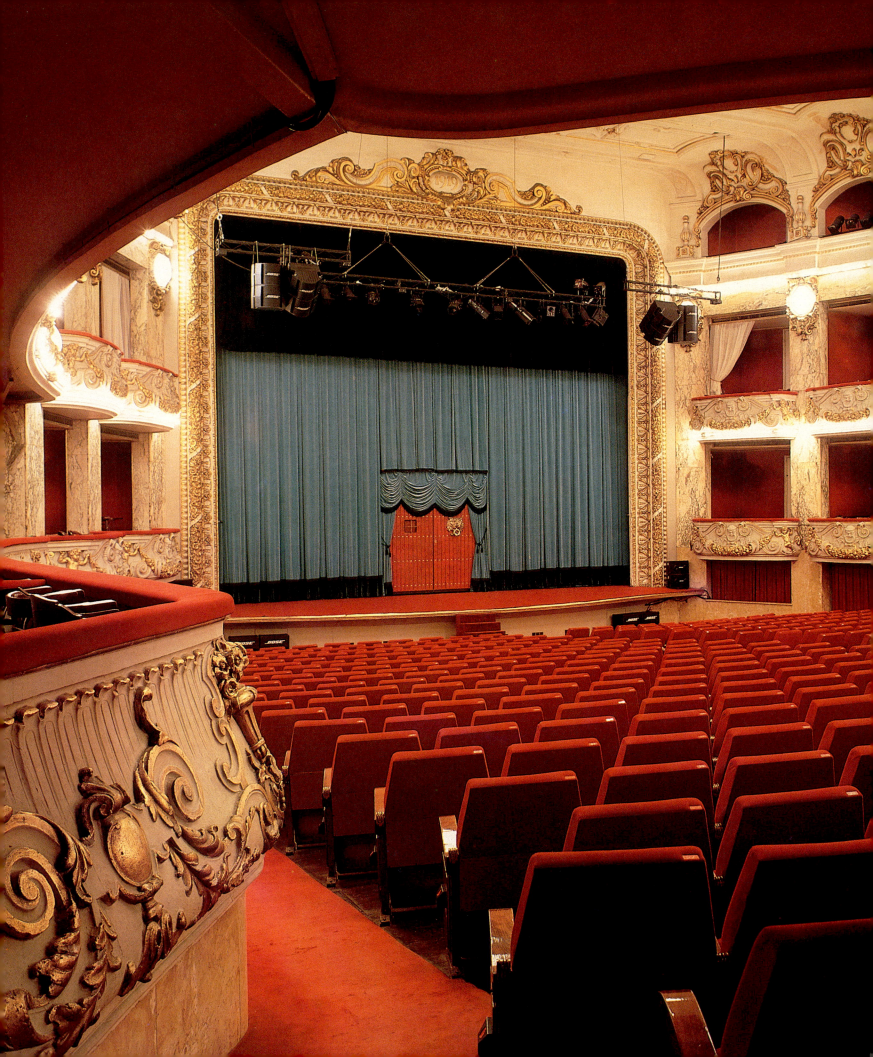

THEATRES, CINEMAS & MUSIC HALLS

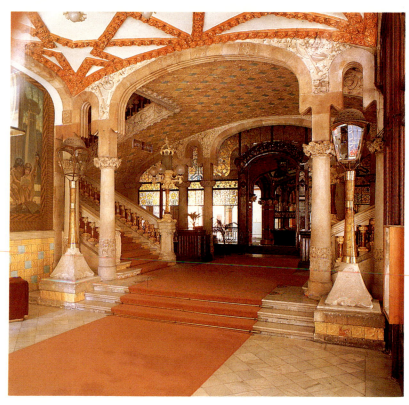

TEATRE TÍVOLI

The original Tívoli Theatre formed part of a complex of leisure facilities located in a large garden to which the inhabitants of Barcelona flocked in their free time. Then it was transferred to its present site in the Carrer Casp where it opened in 1919. For years it was one of the most prestigious cinemas in the city and it continues to be an important one. In the foyer, the imperial staircase with its gilded cast-iron banister leads up to the two tiers of boxes and the gallery. These three levels curve round to form a horseshoe shape which encloses the stalls. From here we can see the complexity of the lavish, carefully executed plaster mouldings, the richness of the gilded trim, and the distinguished appearance of the luxuriously framed stage.

PALAU DE LA MÚSICA CATALANA

Since the turn of the century leading international musicians have come to this concert hall to play. The entrance hall beckons us to explore the treasures within the auditorium where magnificent sculptures by Pablo Gargallo form a backdrop to the players. Under an enormous skylight and with stained-glass side windows, a complicated kaleidoscope of ceramic, glass, marble and iron creates a unique and quite magical combination of colour, shadow and sound. The whole building is a unique delight.

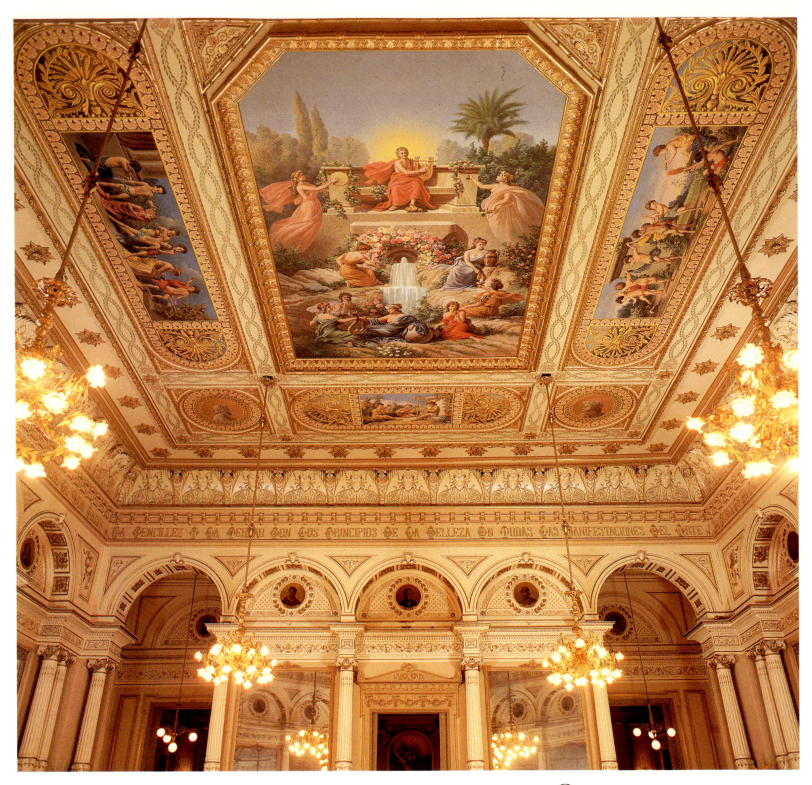

GRAN TEATRE DEL LICEU

*Something very special for Barcelona from the
moment it opened in the mid nineteenth century,
the Gran Teatre del Liceu immediately became
one of the great opera houses of Europe. Not
simply confined to the theatre, performances
became popular social and cultural events and
early this century, as in Salzburg or Bayreuth,
Mozart or Wagner could be found in shops and
offices all over town. Taken from the stage, the
privileged preserve of actors and musicians,
this picture shows the absence of columns*

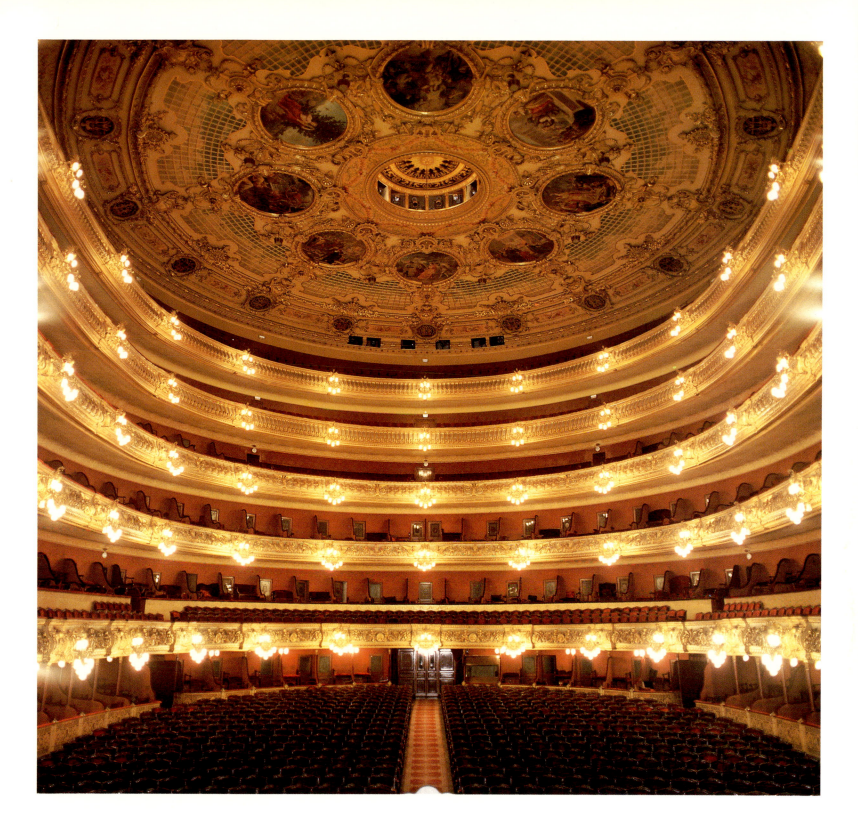

supporting the horseshoe-shaped auditorium's
four levels, which allows a better view from the
sides and lends the interior a grave and elegant
appearance. The skilfully domed ceiling and the
addition of later (1883) Baroque details in the
lamps and fronts of the boxes enhance still
further the beauty of the atmosphere.
In the foyer, known as the Saló dels Miralls
(Hall of Mirrors), the mirrors reflect the gilded
plaster work and the beautiful painted ceiling.

La paloma

*This legendary Barcelona dance hall, even after
so many years still synonymous with glamour
and charm, is said to have derived its name
from the unforgettable* havanera *'La Paloma',
the accompaniment to courtships the world over.
Less poetically, it may have been called after a
night porter's dog at the old ironfoundry on
whose site the dance hall was built.*

*Whichever, many are the loves won and lost in
the golden half-light at La Paloma. Everyone,
from ordinary folk to the glamorous and elegant,
would flood on to the dance floor or gaze at the
nymphs and plaster reliefs and the famous
chandelier, all still in good condition. The city
discovered what a versatile building it is and
today uses the premises as a venue for important
cultural events.*

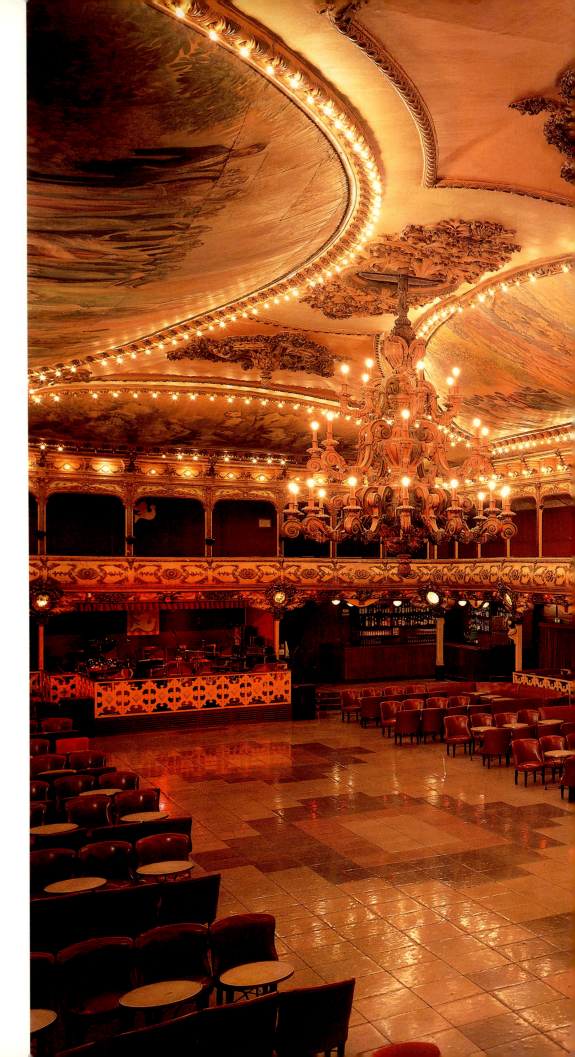

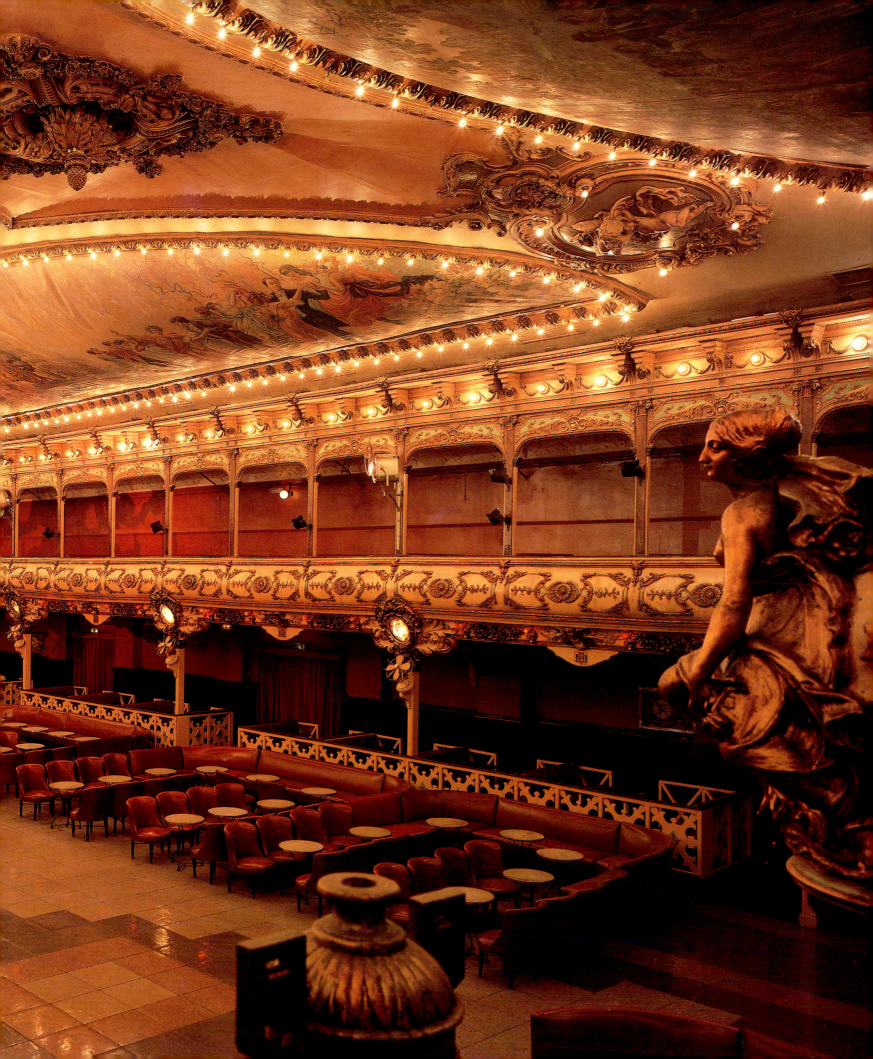

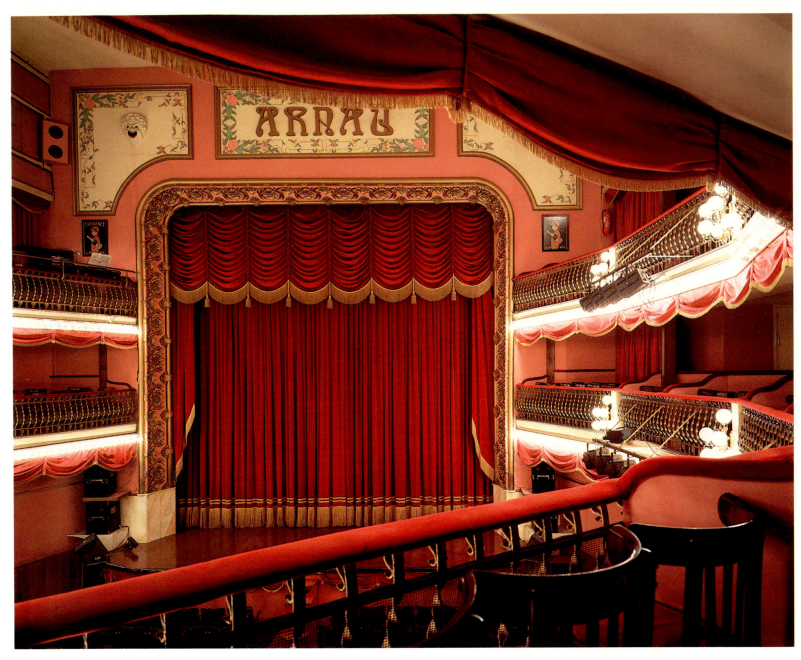

TEATRE ARNAU

On a rather uninspiring street in the heart of the Paral.lel theatre district stands the Teatre Arnau, next to El Molino. Outside it looks like something out of the Wild West and in the not too distant past it was a cinema. Leaving the performance to smoke, talk and laugh in the corridors outside the boxes, the theatre's bourgeois clientele is said to have conducted the odd shady deal in that post-war period when a blind eye was turned to racketeering. In the 1970s the theatre finally became a music hall and now proudly carries on the vaudeville tradition.

EL MOLINO

Barcelona has always had close links with Paris. At the turn of the century a long avenue leading down to the sea became the city's artery of frivolity. In its heyday, the Paral.lel was something like the Boulevard Clichy or Place Pigalle. It was no coincidence that 'La Pajarera', one of the street's most famous variety theatres, soon changed its name to 'Petit-Paris' (1910). Subsequently the modernista architect Raspall put up this building, which became known as The Moulin-Rouge. The Spanish post-war nomenclature, little disposed towards anything foreign, changed it to El Molino (certainly purer but hardly Toulouse-Lautrecian).

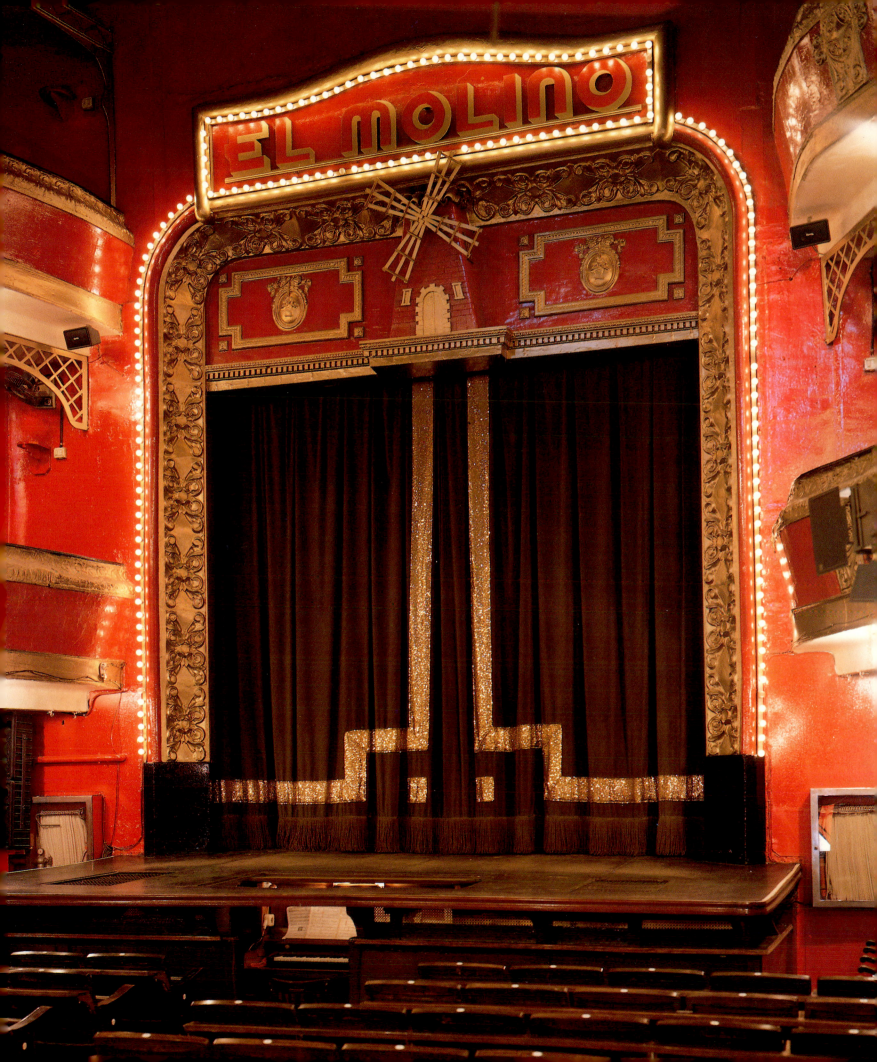

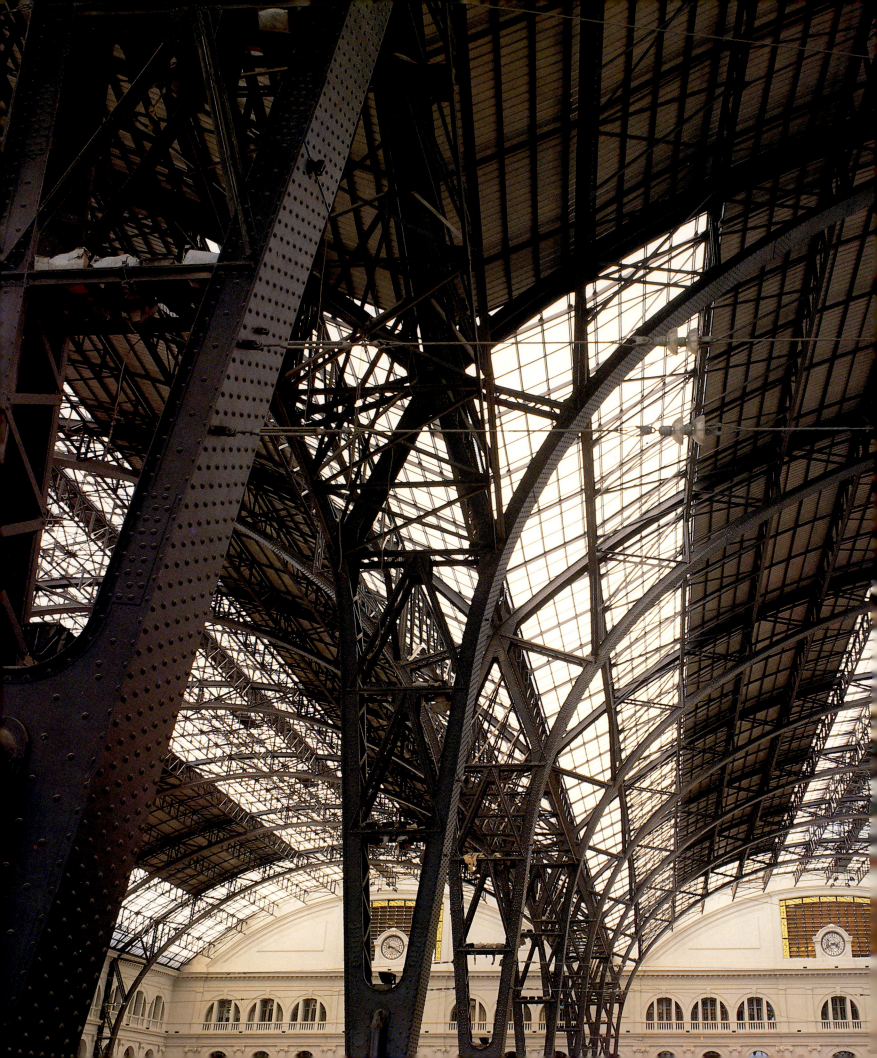

BANKS, OFFICES & STATIONS

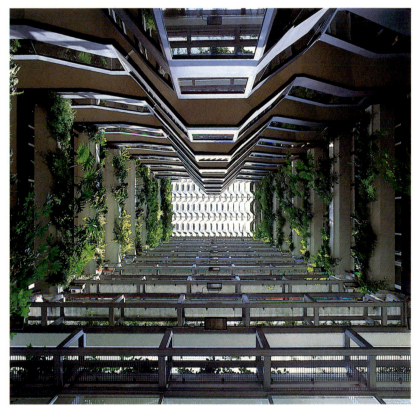

ESTACIÓ DE FRANÇA

At the end of the nineteenth century it became apparent that Barcelona's requirements as a city were ever-increasing. Several proposals for a large-scale station were considered and that by Andreu Montaner, who suggested two gigantic bays with a curved floor plan and laminated iron arches, was the one accepted. At the time of the 1929 International Exhibition it was one of the largest railway terminals in Europe: a grandiose façade, an elegant and spacious entrance hall and two curved vaults protecting the platforms from a height of forty metres.

HERON BUILDING

Until about fifteen years ago country houses stood here, surrounded by vegetable gardens and farms whose cattle supplied milk to many parts of the city. The high-tech Heron Building is one of the giants of Barcelona's new commercial centre. Constructed in 1987-88 it is the happy outcome of a collaborative venture between several prestigious firms of architects. Unique elements are the staircase and this skylight over an interior courtyard filled with greenery.

CONVENTION BUREAU

Barcelona's splendid modernista *architecture is the city's pride and joy and among its best examples is the Casa Lleó i Morera of 1864, one of the oldest houses in the Passeig de Gràcia. Restored by Domènech i Montaner between 1902 and 1906 as a private residence, it now houses the municipal tourist board. Architecture and interior décor are of a piece and of the highest quality. The Gaspar Homar inlaid woodwork, the murals by Josep Pei, mosaics by Mario Maragliano and i Lluis Bru i Selelles, stained glass by Joan Rigalt and Geroni Granell and ceramics by Antoni Serra i Fiter combine to make a small treasure house of Catalan* Modernisme.

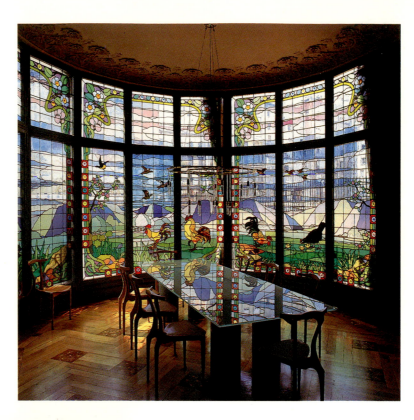

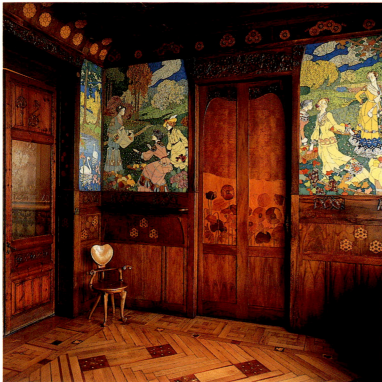

BANCA CATALANA

Built in 1874 as the head office of the Banca Mas Sardà, one of Catalonia's most prestigious banking establishments at the turn of the century, later this building housed a jeweller's much frequented by the ladies of Barcelona. Its present owners, the Banca Catalana, have restored it to its original use: the intricate woodwork, etched glass, marble and brass conjure up all the atmosphere of the fin de siècle. *With just a little imagination you can still hear the ring of the carriage wheels and smell the flowers on the world-famous avenue La Rambla.*

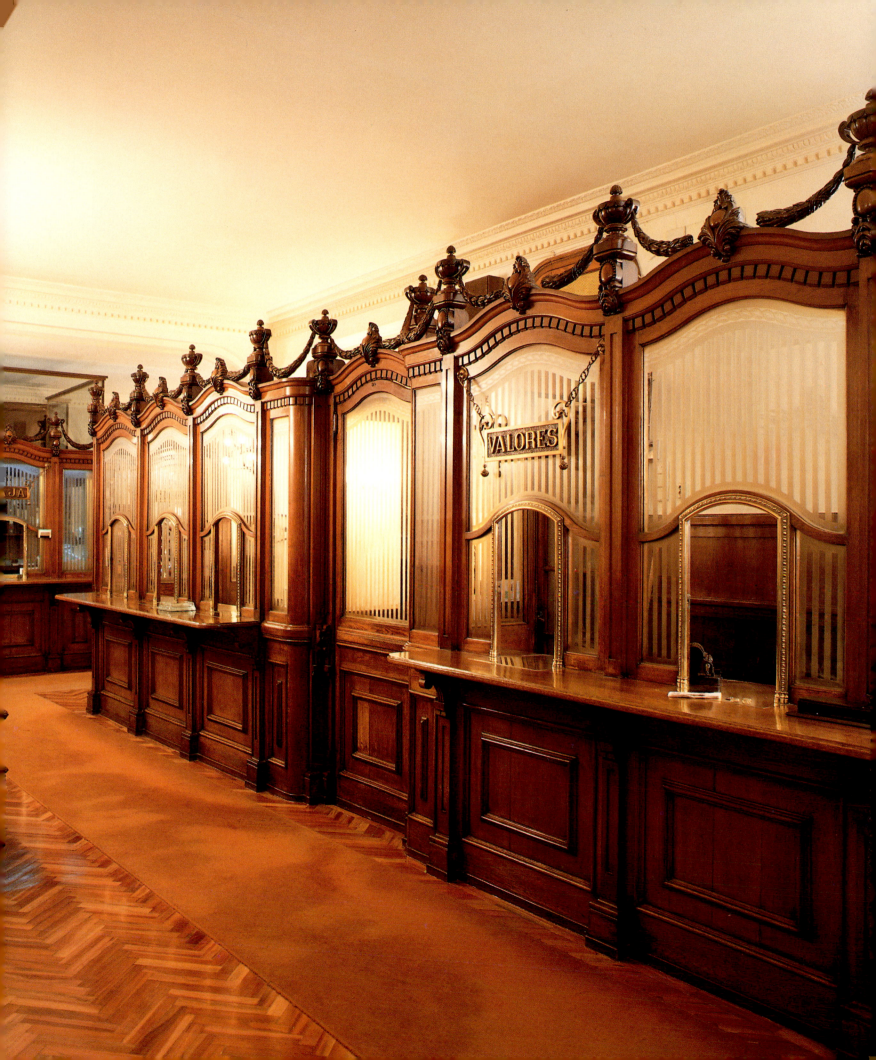

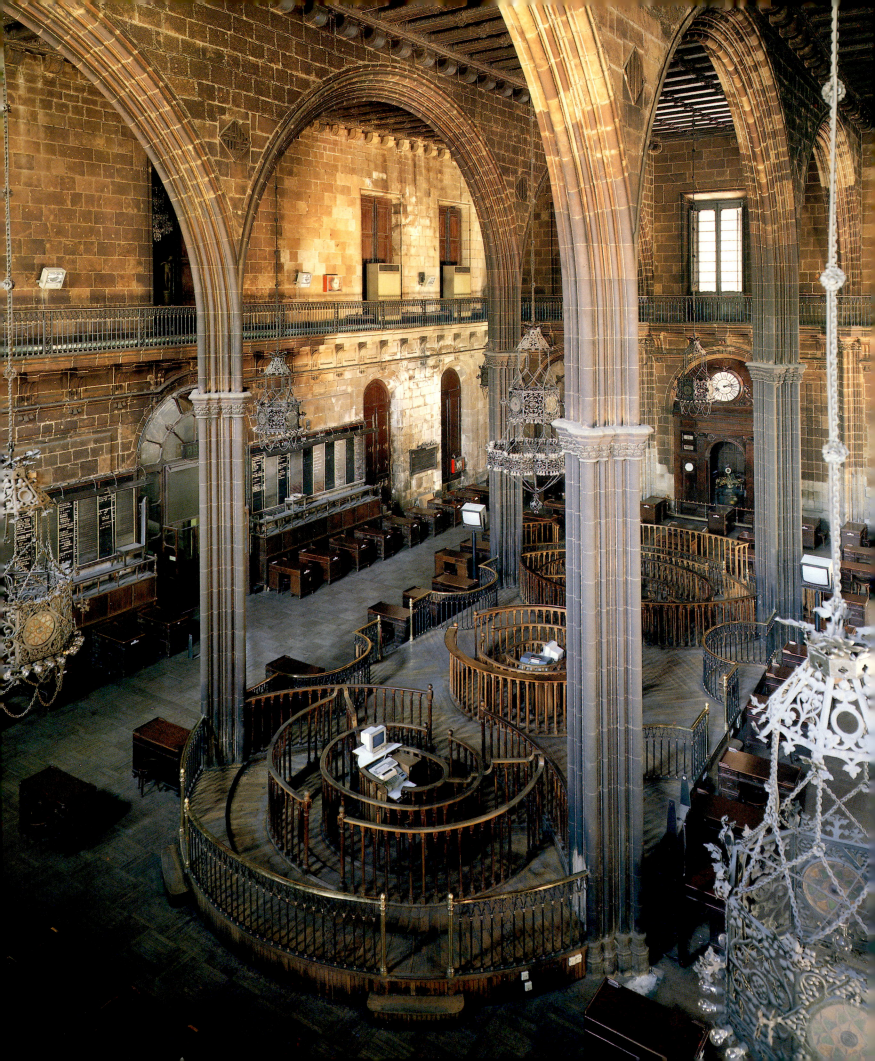

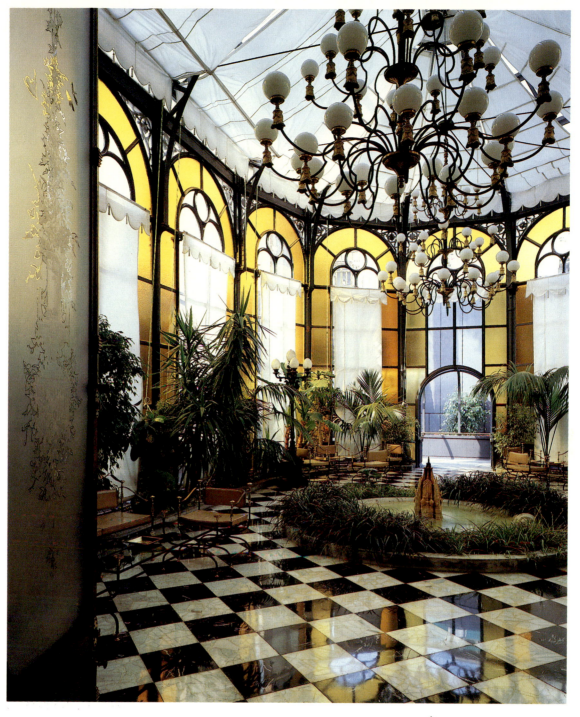

Llotja

This splendid medieval Catalan gothic interior was until recently the Barcelona Stock Exchange. It was built in 1383 by Pere Arbei as the 'Saló de Contractació', and consists of tall, elegant pillars and diaphragmatic arches which support the polychromatic ceiling, producing a sensation of great amplitude and beauty.

Aigües de Barcelona

A few decades ago, Barcelona's municipal water company took over one of the big houses built by the Catalan bourgeoisie in the right side of the Eixample (an area not unlike London's Mayfair). The original spirit of a private house was preserved and its magnificent conservatory rebuilt. Under a roof supported by fine columns and cast-iron arches, stands a small fountain with a finely worked marble sculpture of two Tritons.

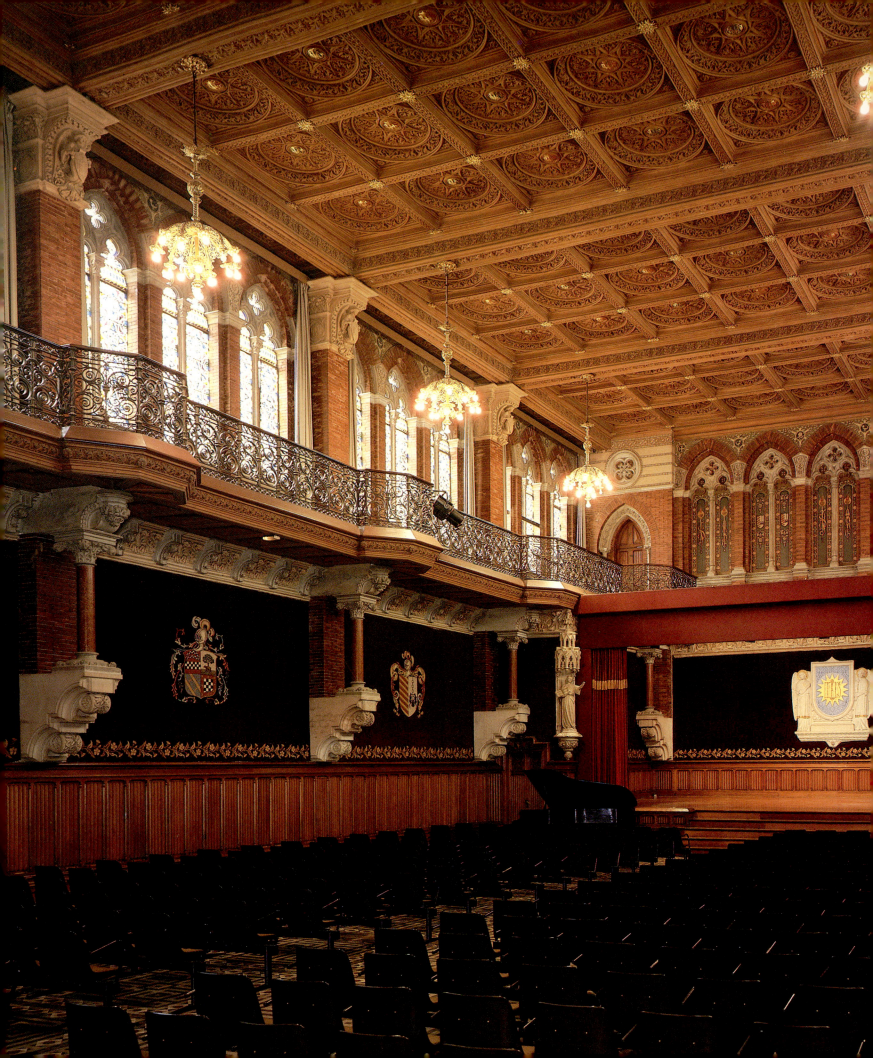

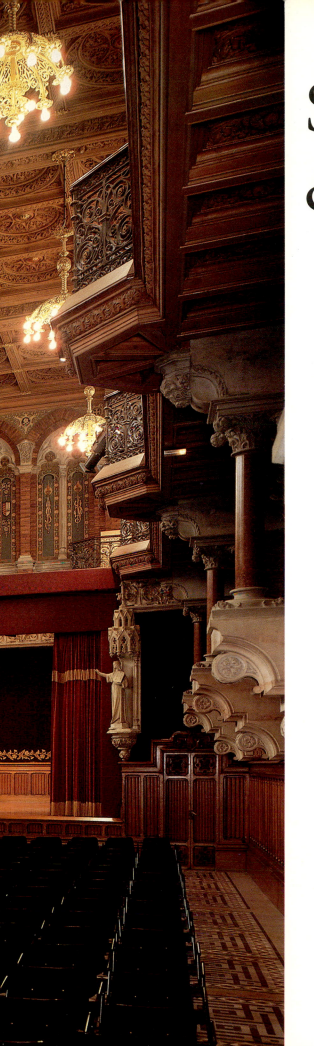

SCHOOLS
& COLLEGES

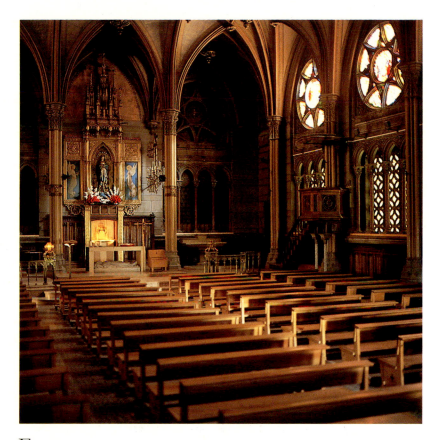

Escola dels Jesuïtes de Sarrià

Like other religious orders looking for better climatic conditions in which to site their schools, the Jesuits of Sarrià built theirs on the slope of the Tibidabo mountain. Planned as a boarding school, it is like an English college in layout and external appearance. This lecture hall with its neo-Gothic windows is richly decorated, expressing something of the importance and exclusive character of the building. Especially notable are the floor which is composed of small bits of gres, the highly decorative ceiling, the fine white stonework on the capitals and the wrought-iron banisters.

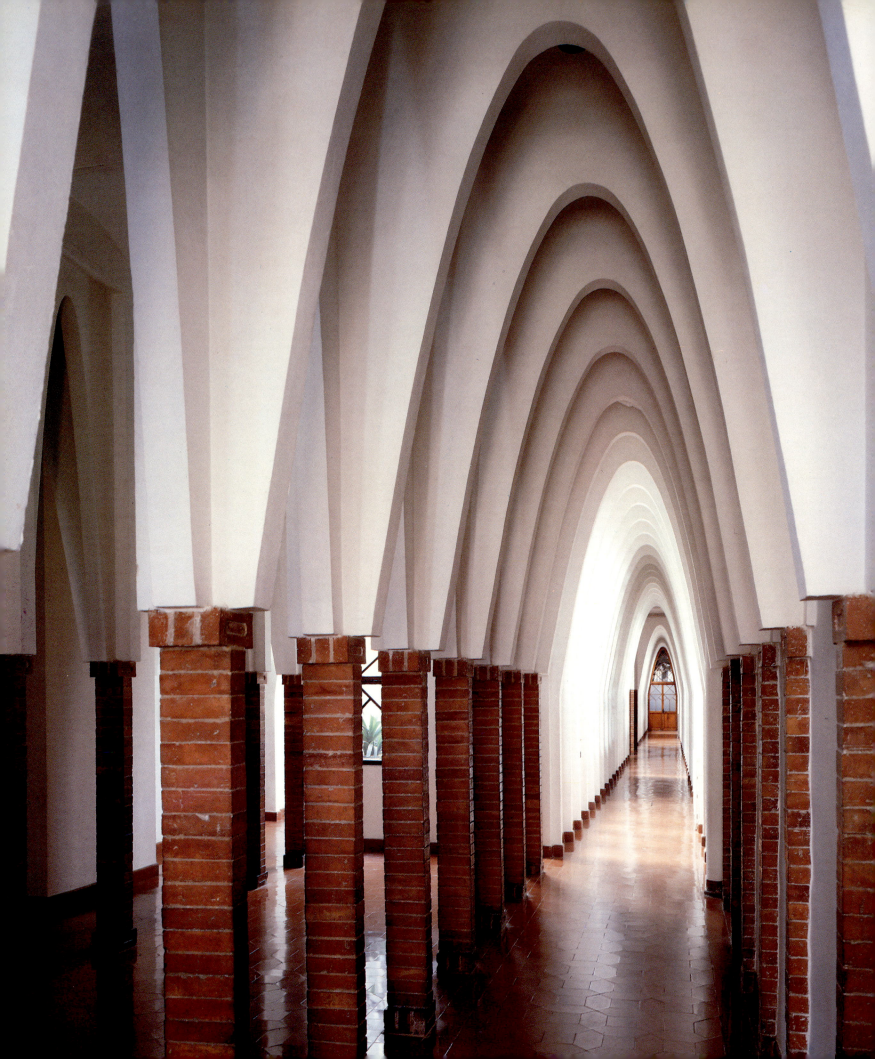

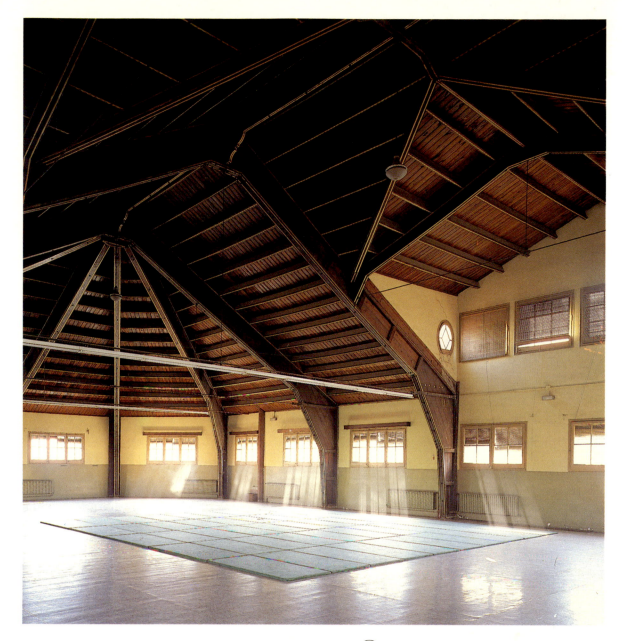

GRUP ESCOLAR PERE VILA

In the early 1930s Barcelona City Council implemented a programme of educational reform, encouraged by Prat de la Riba, President of the Mancomunitat de Catalunya. Forty new schools were constructed, many built by the council architect Josep Goday i Casals, and all were faithful to the aesthetic and conceptual ideas of Noucentisme, seen here in the Mediterranean Baroque style of the painter Francesc Canyelles' graffito and ceramic relief work. This contrasts with the calm strength of the architect's construction techniques and treatment of large spaces. His use of form and control of light are inspirational, as in the all-purpose hall - maybe gymnasium, chapel or assembly hall.

COL·LEGI DE LES TERESIANES

It may have been no bad thing that the precarious funds available for the construction of this school put the brake on Gaudí's exuberant creativity. Respecting the need for economy he restricted himself to an austere and rigorous design, yet the building's apparent monotony of construction conceals special and unexpected wealth. With his customary boldness, Gaudí moved the interior load-bearing walls from floor to floor and thus achieved a majestic cascade of light through the roof. The tunnels formed by the parabolic arches which he uses to achieve the effect are bathed in a diffuse light which accentuates the convent's introverted and spiritual character.

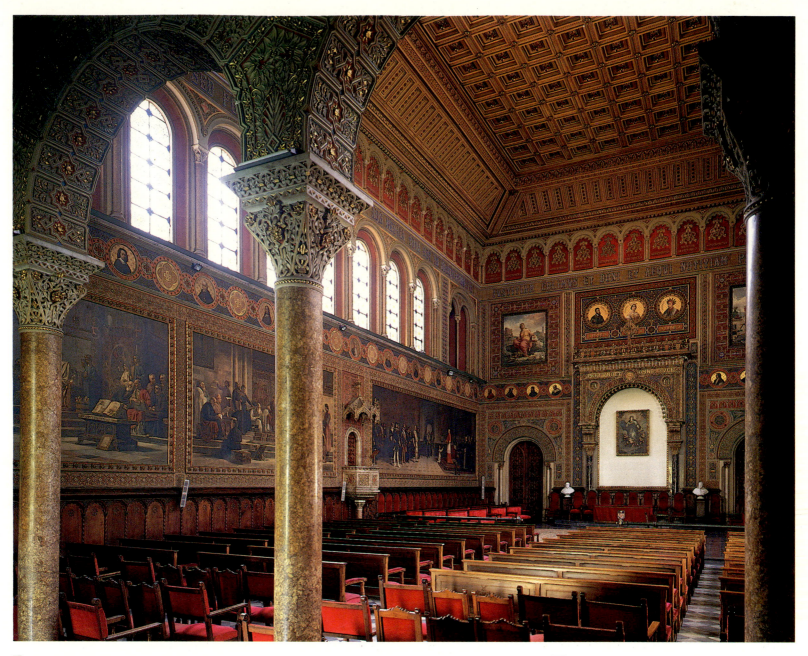

PARANIMF DE LA UNIVERSITAT CENTRAL DE BARCELONA

Viollet-le-Duc, with the usual rationalism which implies the use of different styles so as to avoid strict academicism, came to Catalonia through Elies Rogent and the University of Barcelona, a solemn neo-Romanesque building, and it is specifically in the Paranimf - in which university ceremonies take place - that these ideas can be most clearly appreciated: Byzantine, mozarabic and all other classical motifs are present, but the most important is the way all are used as a manifestation of the true history of Catalonia.

ESCOLA DEL TREBALL

The vigour and importance of Catalan industrial life at the end of the nineteenth century are still clearly expressed in this building which stands on the site of an embroidery factory designed in 1860 by Rafael Guastavino.
In 1927 Joan Rubió i Bellvé built his new School of Engineering here. The entrance hall, seen here, has a spectacular structure of parabolic arches supporting a stepped roof in which lateral series of windows create a light source of great beauty. The position of the bricks in the arches and the use of ceramics as dividers between them are worth emphasizing, as are the polychromatic wooden ceiling and the graffiti on the walls, which have more of a feeling of Noucentisme than of Modernisme where chronologically they belong.

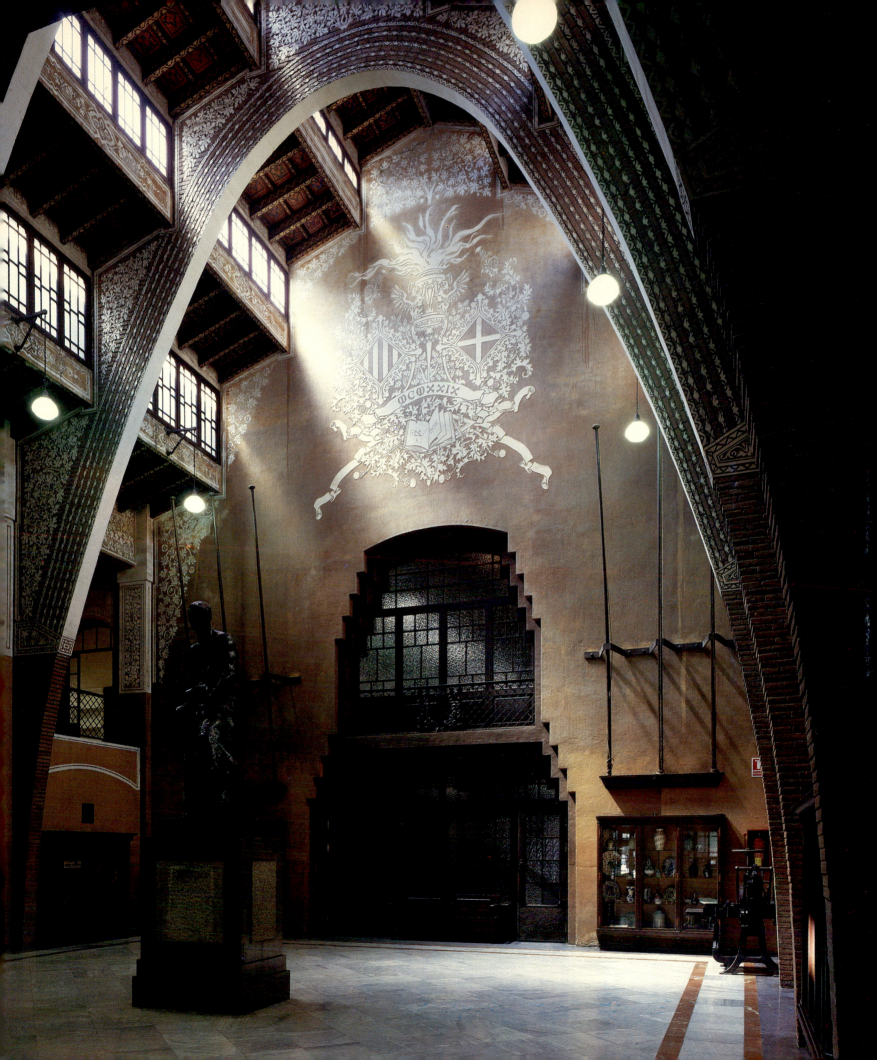

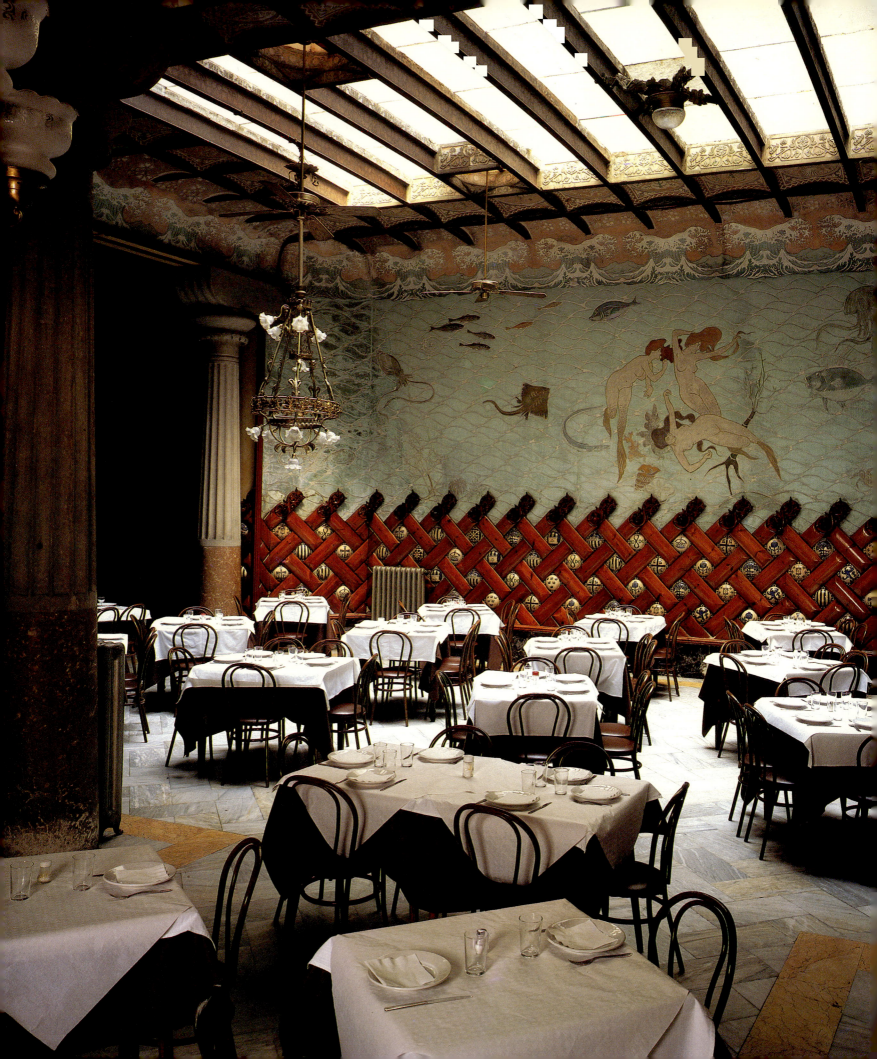

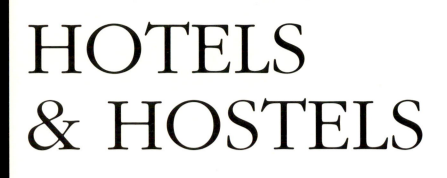

HOTELS
& HOTELS

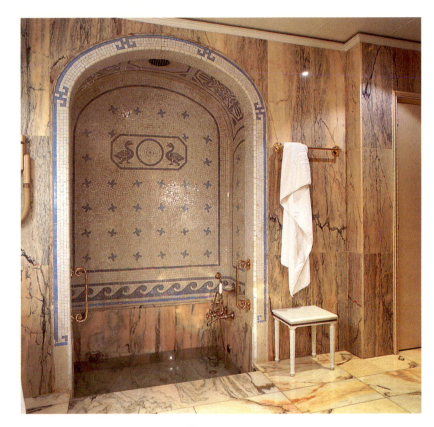

HOTEL ESPAÑA

A sort of Sistine Chapel among Barcelona's hotels, the Hotel España had to put up with the prudery of the post-war period which insisted on covering up with white paint the naked nymphs swimming in this great mural in the dining room. In spite of this the hotel is still a masterpiece among modernista *interiors.*
Built in 1900, responsibility for the interior decoration was entrusted to Domènech i Montaner who shared the work with Eusebi Arnau.
The degradation of the building continued at the hands of later owners. With the advent of democracy at least the nymphs were unveiled to dance once more in complete freedom.

HOTEL RITZ

What songs the tiles in this marble bathroom of the Ritz's royal suite might sing in praise of beauties who have bathed here like Aegean goddesses! Ava Gardner was one. Two steps lead down to the mosaic-lined sunken bath. In the sumptuous bedroom, connected to the reception room, extravagantly luxurious curtains hide the large bed in this the hotel's biggest suite.

ALBERG MARE DE DÉU DEL COLL

This elaborate, neo-Arabian entrance hall was constructed at a time when the Near East meant everything to do with exoticism and enchantment. The large Modernista house, originally the summer home of a prominent bourgeois family called the Marsans, was built in 1907. During the Civil War it housed the social services department and subsequently became a convent and orphanage until converted into a youth hostel in 1983.

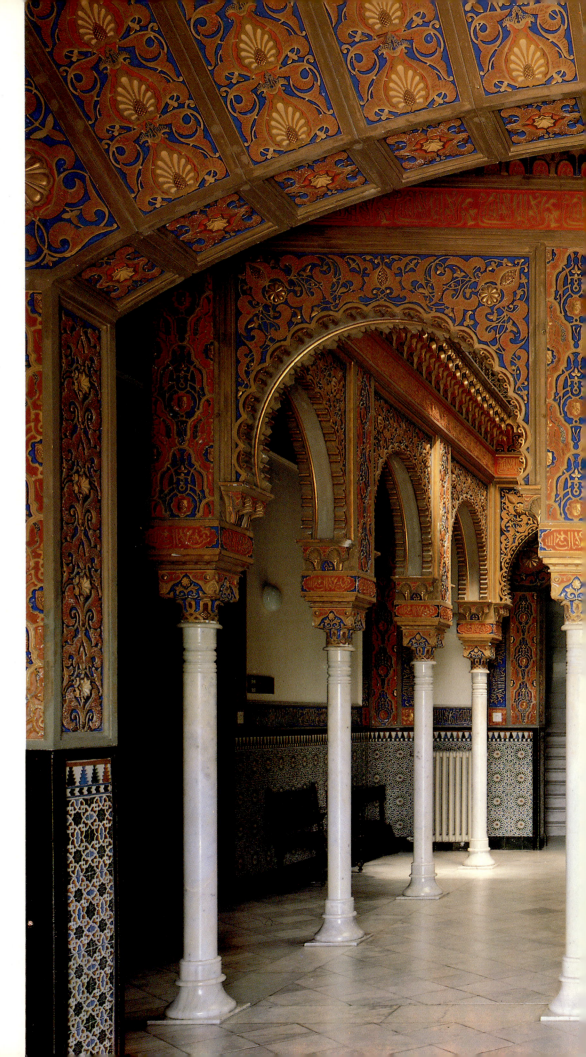

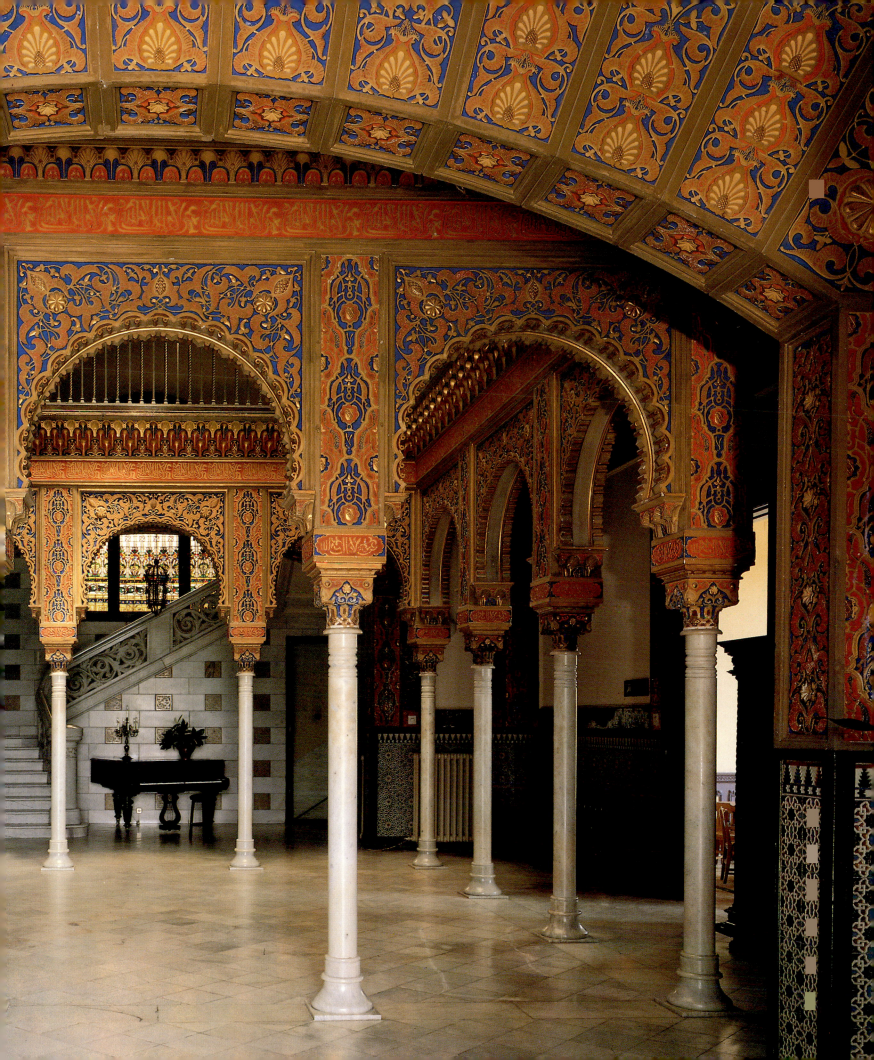

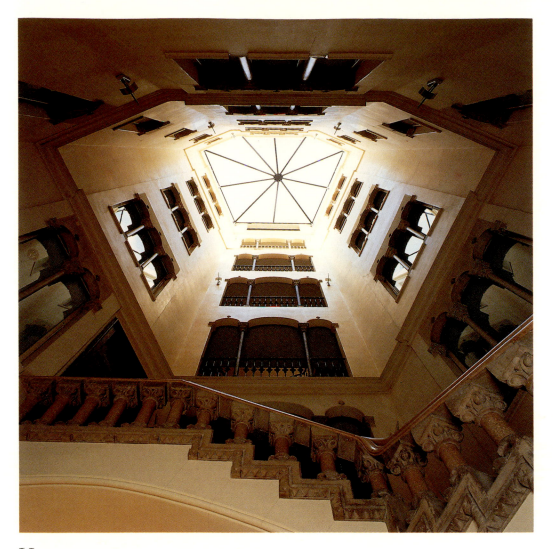

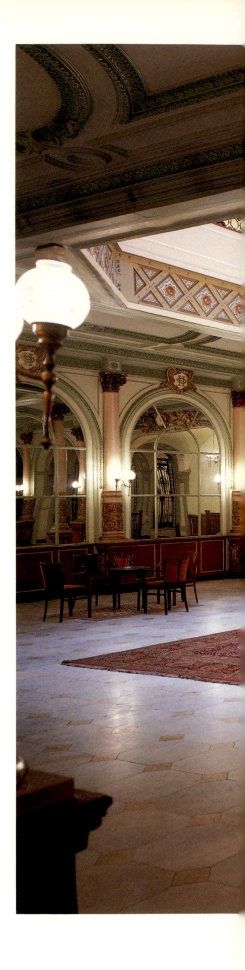

HOTEL COMTES DE BARCELONA

*The Passeig de Gràcia where this hotel stands
still has all the splendour that the Catalan
upper middle classes gave it at the turn of the
century. Once a private residence it is a great
triumph when buildings like this have been able
to change use without losing their original
glamour.*

HOTEL ORIENTE

*The enigmatic Hotel Oriente was chosen by the
film director Antonioni as the setting for scenes
in his oppressive dramas of non-communication
such as* The Reporter. *Even in the last
century it ranked among the great European
hotels. The original structure, a school built by
the Franciscans in 1652, has been retained -
what were once the cloisters are now the hotel
ballroom. Perhaps Antonioni chose this building
with so much history to emphasize the
unhappiness of a hero without past or identity.*

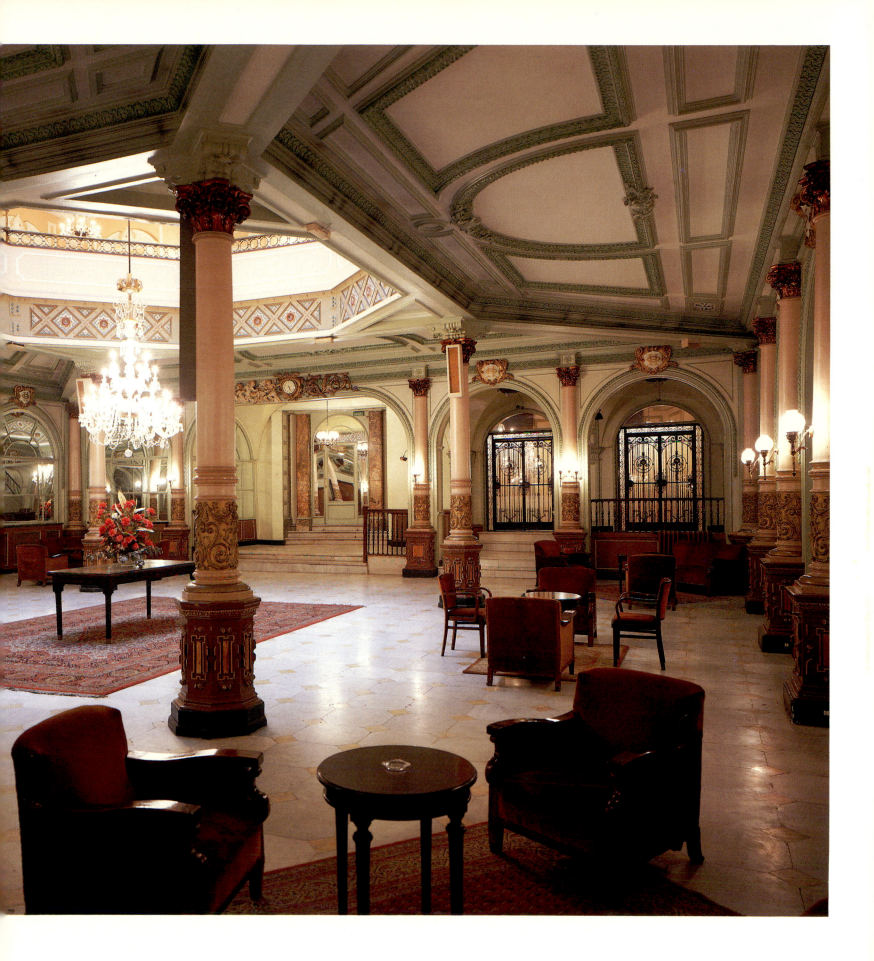

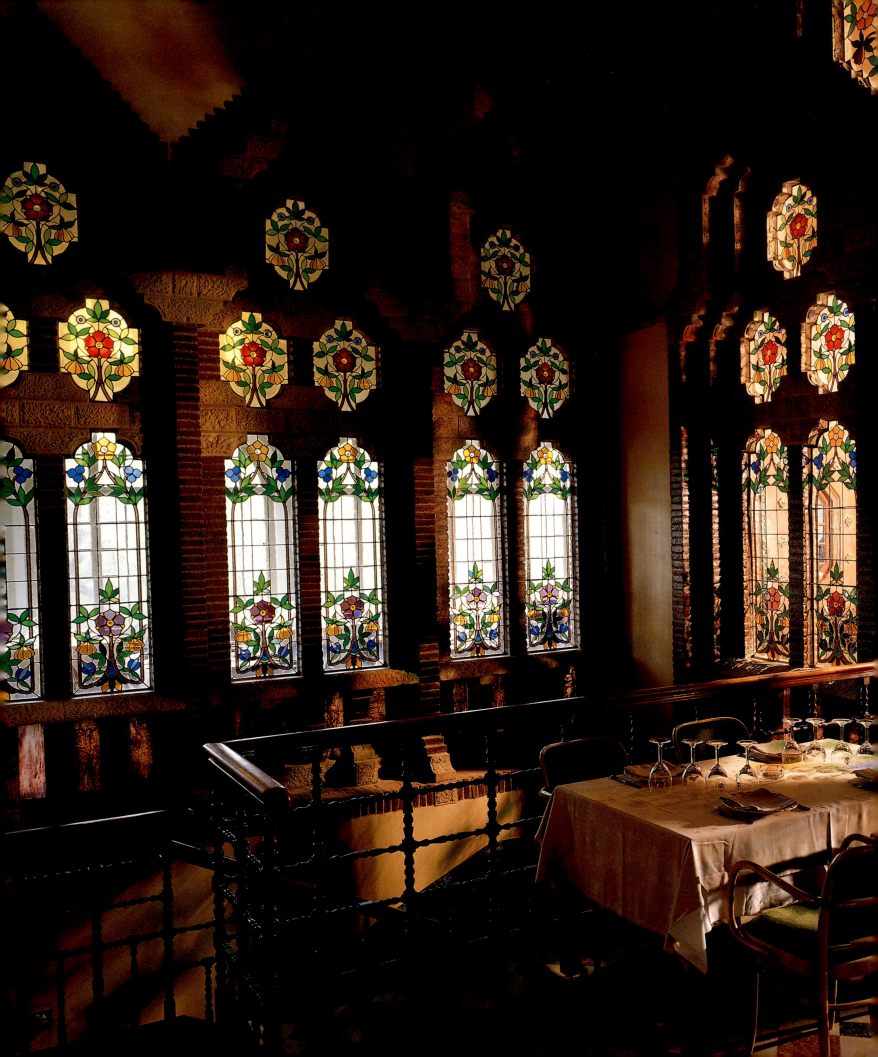

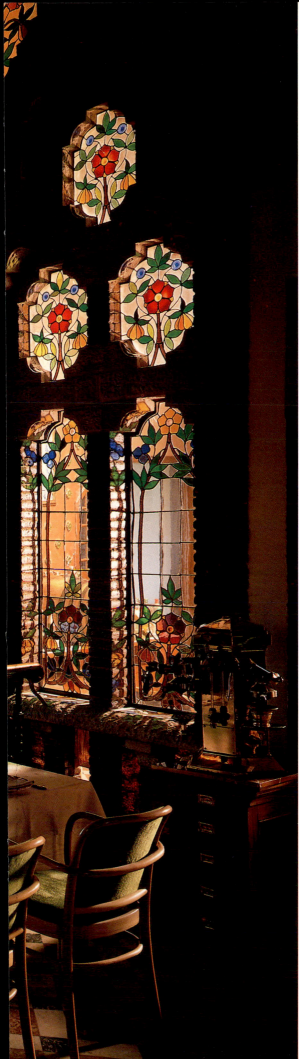

BARS & RESTAURANTS

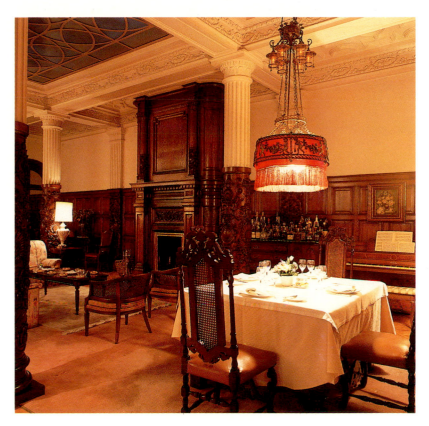

EL FRARE BLANC (EL ASADOR DE ARANDA)

This elegant example of Modernisme *in a private house was designed in 1903 by Joan Rubió i Bellvé for the Roviralta family. One of a row of houses with gardens it is brick built with arches, eaves and an attic storey of great virtuosity. The wrought-iron work is especially skilful and the stained glass through which light filters on to the tables of what is now a restaurant is a delight. The house was constructed on the site of an old Dominican convent, hence the name 'The White Friar'.*

BELTXENEA

The dining room and upper rooms of this house are now a most refined restaurant, with cuisine and service to match in perfection. The fireplace in the elegant old dining room serves to remind us of the well-being and cultural richness of a certain class and epoch in Barcelona, reflected in the sense of luxury in space and ornamentation found in the domestic architecture.

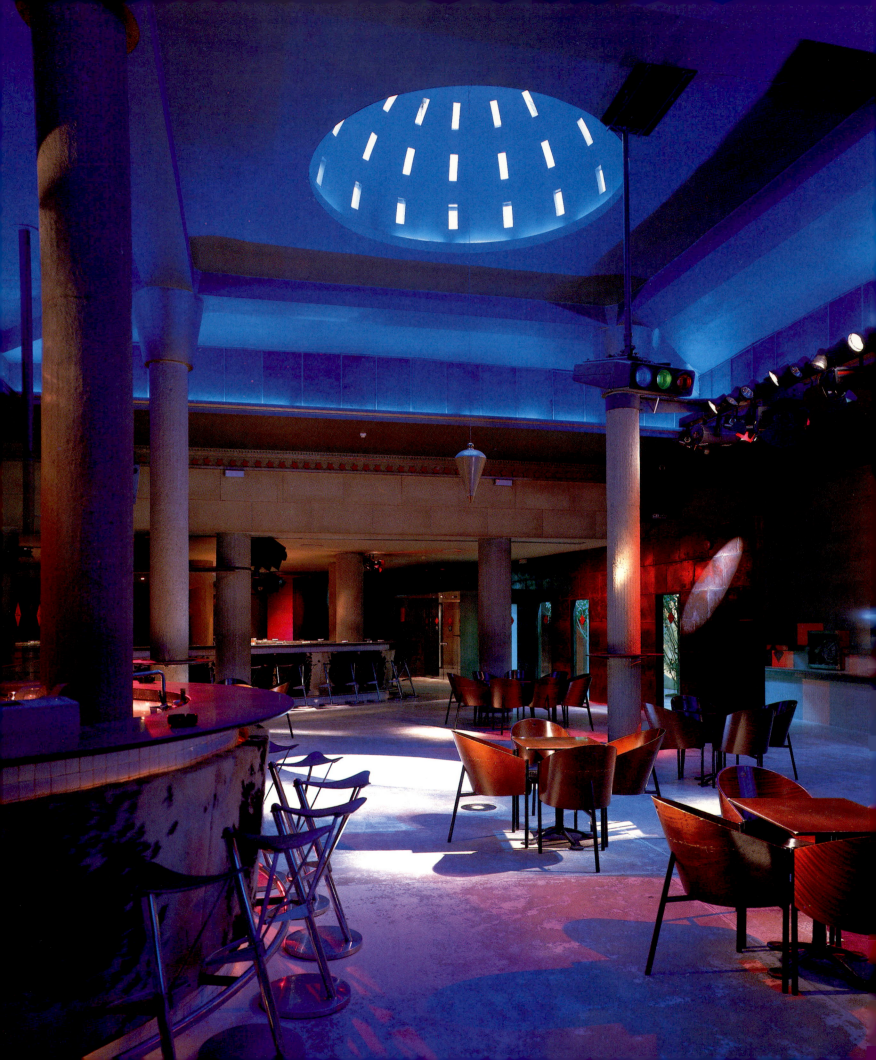

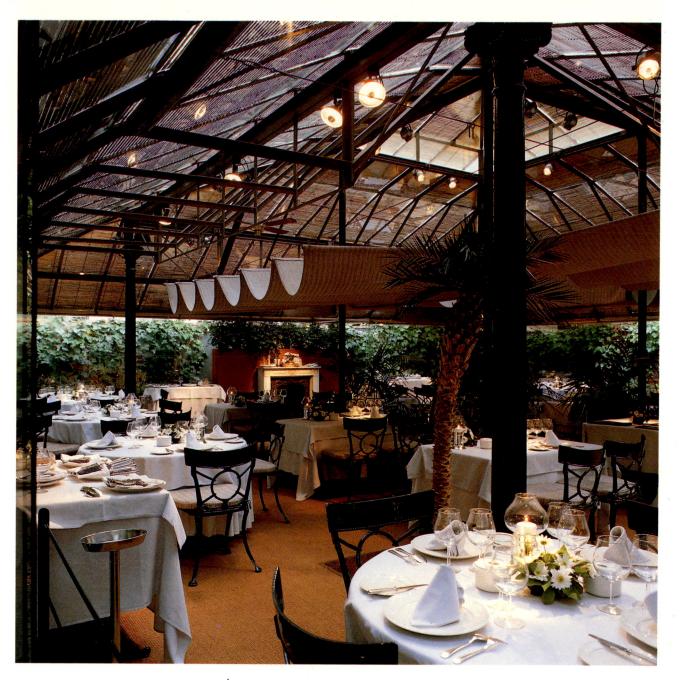

AZULETE

Barcelona boasts various establishments where the good cooking is matched by sumptuous surroundings. This restaurant's garden dining room is reached through the ground floor of an old modernista villa. A place to eat in great comfort, it is like being in a conservatory under the vaulted glass roof.

NICK HAVANNA

Don't be surprised by the impressive finish and the startling play of water sliding over the mirrored ceiling in the cloakroom at the Nick Havanna. These are just two of the unusual elements which 'new design' has employed in the furthest corner of this bar. Created in 1986, other outstanding design features at this nightspot are its mobile bar, side tiers, cupola and pendulum, and a video wall which projects the same image on each of its dozens of gleaming eyes. Since it opened, the Nick Havanna has become one of Barcelona's most attractive venues.

BRASSERIE FLO

Although located in a nineteenth-century building, this restaurant was designed after the style of French turn-of-the-century brasseries. There are interesting details to be found, such as the combination of Catalan modernista *motifs and secessionist elements. The overall effect is of a comfortable space, ideal for enjoying a late supper after attending a concert in the nearby Palau de la Música. Warm reminders of Bertolucci will delight the cinephile - sober colours and smooth spheres of light. The lighting might have been done by Storaro and would please Coppola himself.*

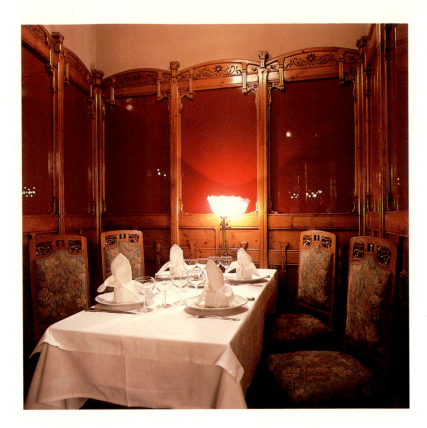

VELÒDROM

This run-down 1940s bar was miraculously saved from demolition by speculators, a fate which had seemed inevitable but which was avoided thanks to the 1976 Pla General *which altered the site's planning consent. Time has darkened its walls and worn its furniture, but few bars in Barcelona attract such a disparate clientele throughout the day. A discreetly Bohemian community rubs shoulders with impeccably attired young designers. At the back of the room billiards players are engrossed in interminable games. In the gallery the older patrons play cards, or sit and dream, perhaps of their first loves. In short, at the Velòdrom time is relative and takes on a quality of its own.*

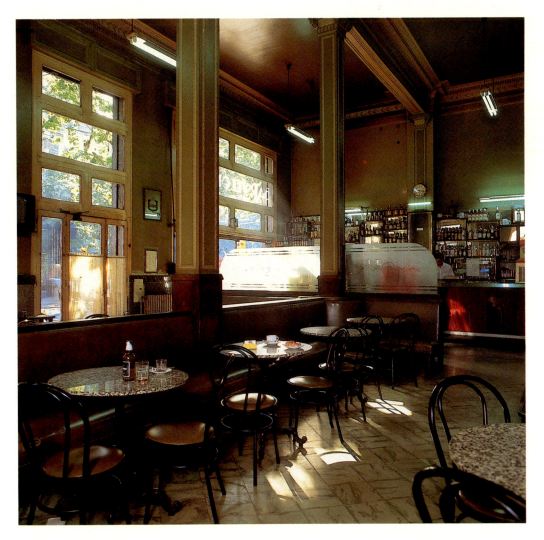

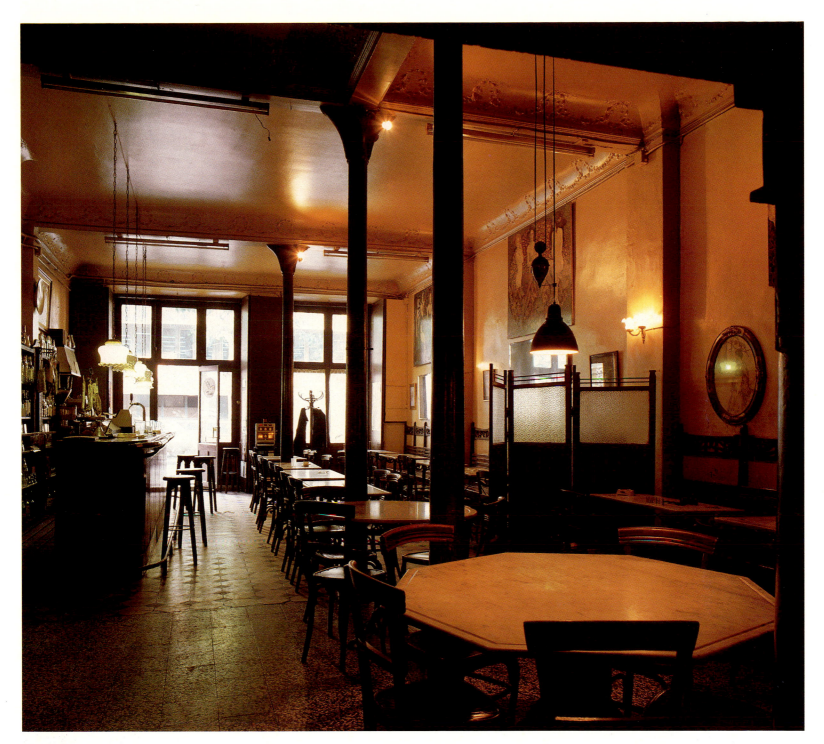

CAFE DEL CENTRE

During the Republic (1931-36) the Café del Centre in the elegant Eixample quarter was known as a smart gambling spot. Large fortunes were undoubtedly lost by some of the casino's wealthy patrons, many of them members of the textile bourgeoisie. With the prohibition of gambling the casino was turned into a bodega and café, but the café has kept the table where 'l'Avi' (Grandfather) Bel, a legendary croupier, set himself up as the herald of fortune.

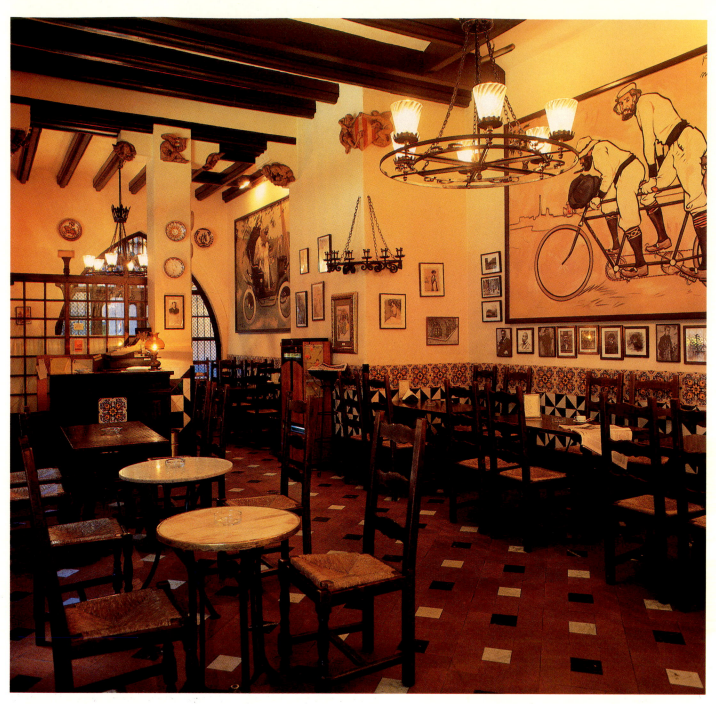

ELS QUATRE GATS

With echoes of Parisian artistic cafés, this was Puig i Cadafalch's first important work. Neo-Gothic in concept, visible in the composition and ornamentation, elements of popular Catalan architecture and the nascent modernista style are freely incorporated. For years the café was to Barcelona what Le Lapin Agile was for Paris: a meeting place for young and restless creators of the avant-garde. Numerous well-known artists of the period came here to exhibit. Indeed Els Quatre Gats was Picasso's first platform. Happily restored, the café is a shrine to twentieth-century art, to a time when painters would theorize in cafés such as this before returning to the solitude of the studio to complete their works.

LOS CARACOLES

Long before it got its name this busy restaurant was a shop selling everything. So popular were the snails with the customers who stood at the counter to eat tapas *that in 1915 the shop became known as Los Caracoles - The Snails'. Its conversion into a restaurant was greeted with enthusiasm and people flocked here from the literary, artistic and film worlds.*
The owners - the Bofarull brothers - have maintained good relationships with all their customers, even helping to defray the costs of Buñuel's first films.

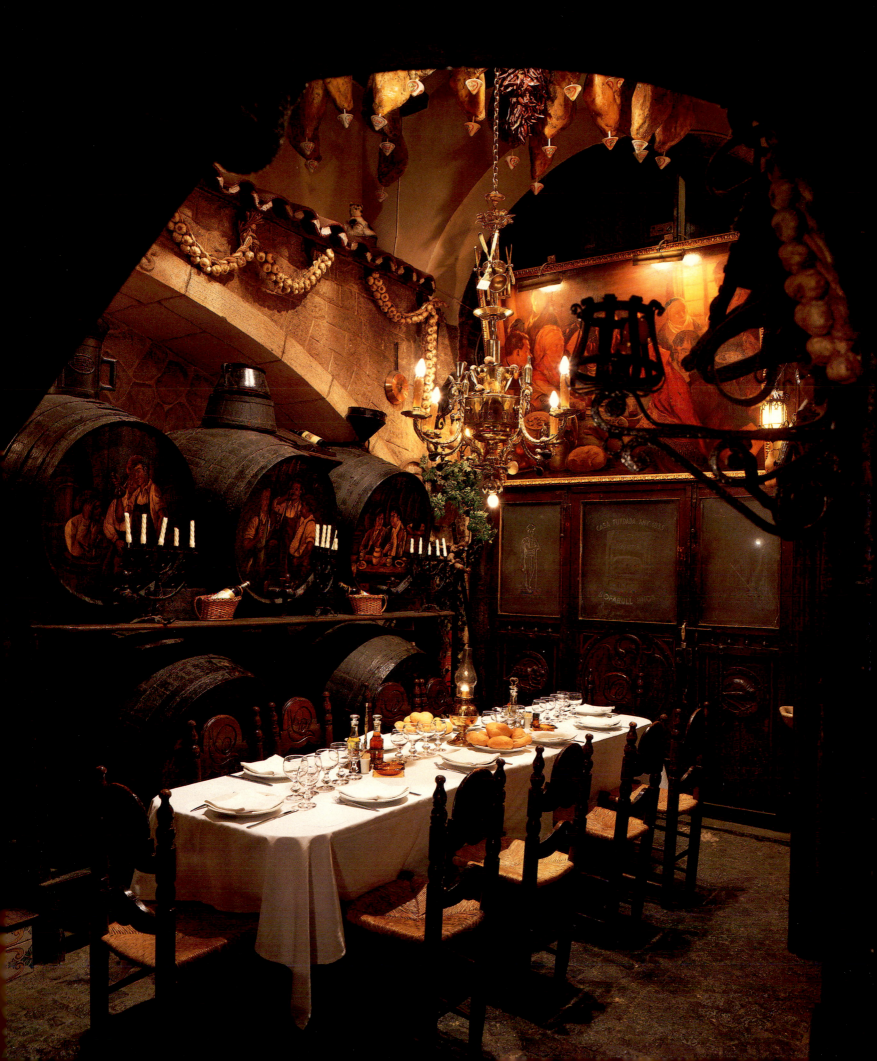

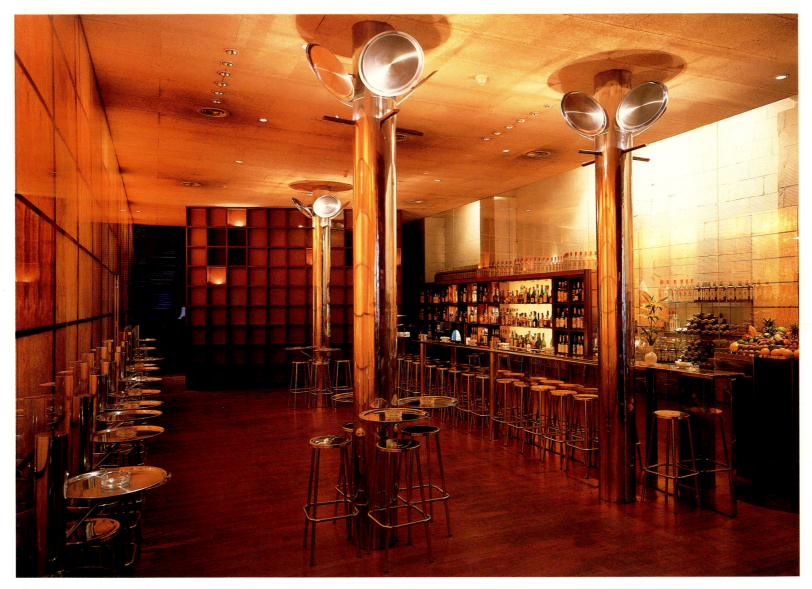

ZSA-ZSA

Should fortune smile on you, perhaps the great cocktail-maker Ginés, one of the glories of the young cocktail scene, will prepare you an unforgettable mixture. Savour your drink as you stand by the marvellous translucent wall, made of birchwood; in this modern bar light is the leitmotiv.

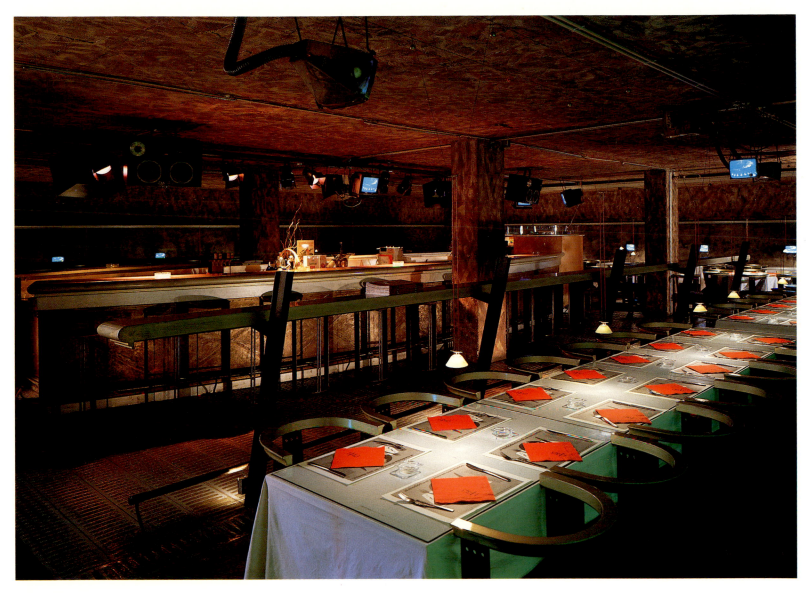

NETWORK

This new concept in bar-restaurants appeared in Barcelona in the late 1980s. The entrance, with its hanging moon and great globe of the earth, conveys an atmosphere of icy warmth reminiscent of futuristic movies like Blade Runner. *And although you may not be Harrison Ford, you might just find your 'replicant' here.*

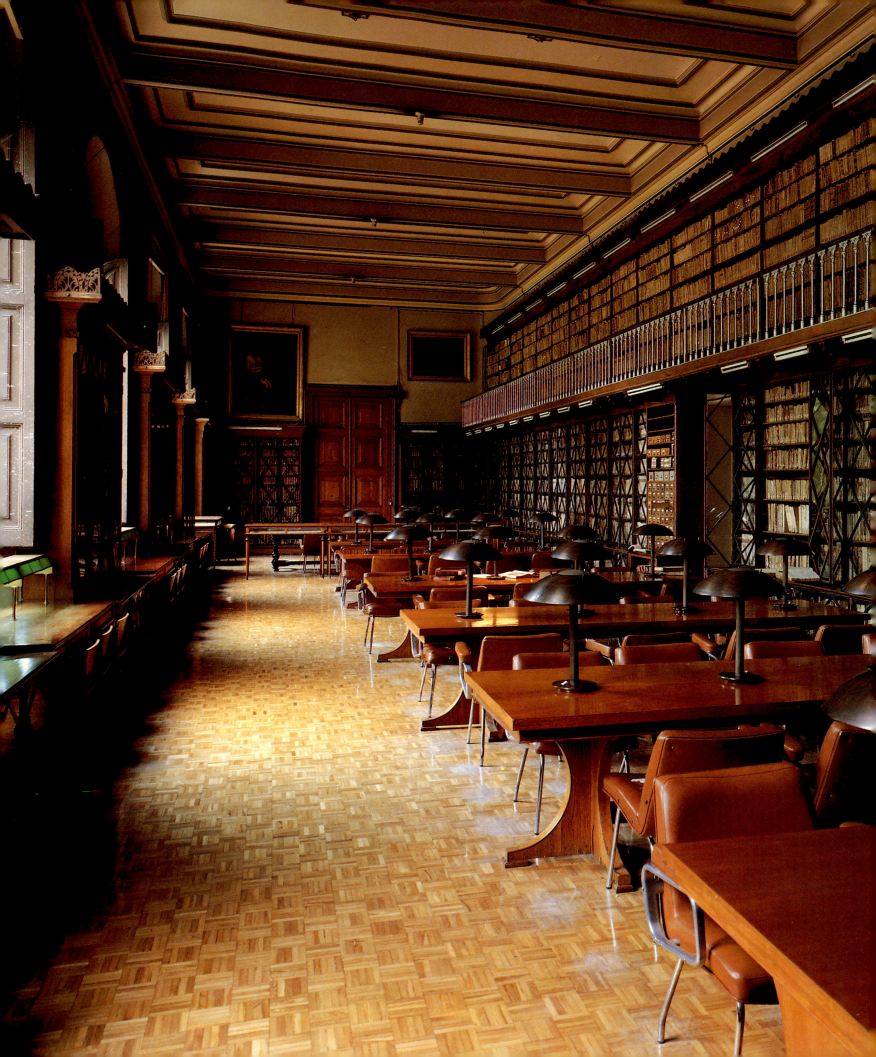

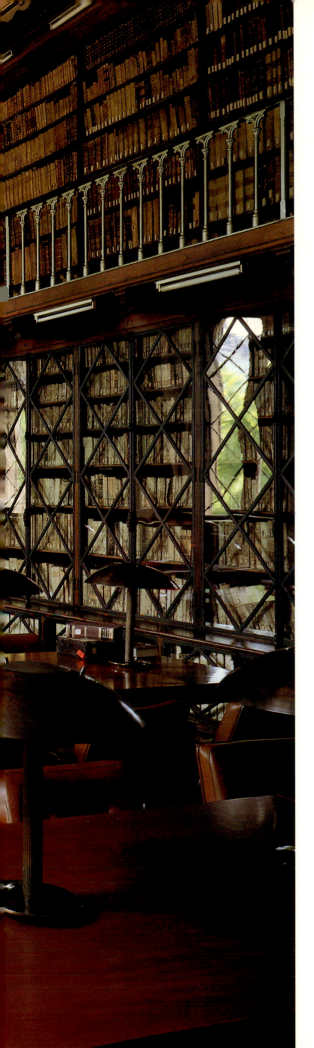

LIBRARIES & ARCHIVES

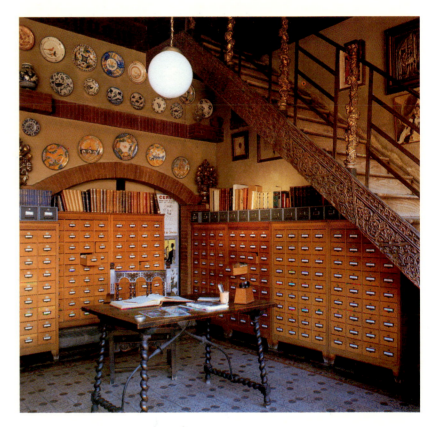

BIBLIOTECA DE LA UNIVERSITAT

*Located in the old university, this building was
designed and furnished by Elies Rogent.
The library itself was planned later by Josep
Gonzàlez and Francesc Perales, the latter being
freer in outlook than the former. The entire
building exudes monumentalism; typical is the
use of iron in the structure. Near here Victoria
de los Angeles sang her first notes and many are
the eminent scholars who have passed through
these rooms.*

ARXIU FOTOGRÀFIC MAS

*Every one of these small drawers contains a
piece of Catalonia's history, Barcelona's in
particular. Hardly surprising, then, that this
photographic archive is the place above all others
to which one turns to do one's research. Under
the generous supervision of its curators out glides
the photographic record of our past - silent
images perfectly ordered.*

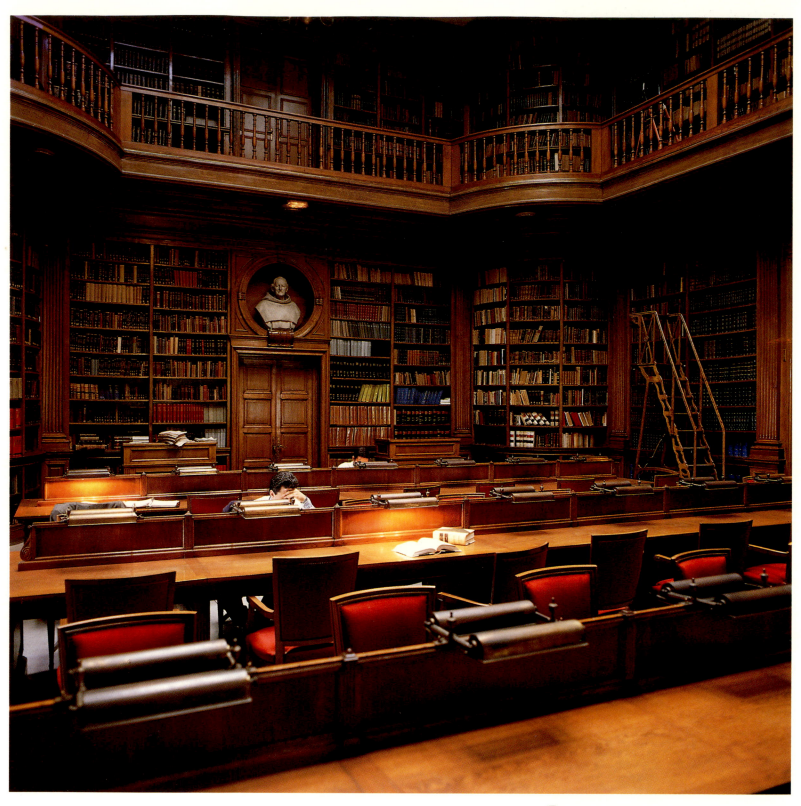

BIBLIOTECA DEL COLLEGI D'ADVOCATS

All that lawyers need to know of the complex world of laws regulating human conduct can be found in this calm and sheltered sanctuary within the Palau Cassades. The thousands of books set in hundreds of skilfully designed shelves, rhythmically surrounding the room, create just the conducive atmosphere needed for research into the secrets of human behaviour.

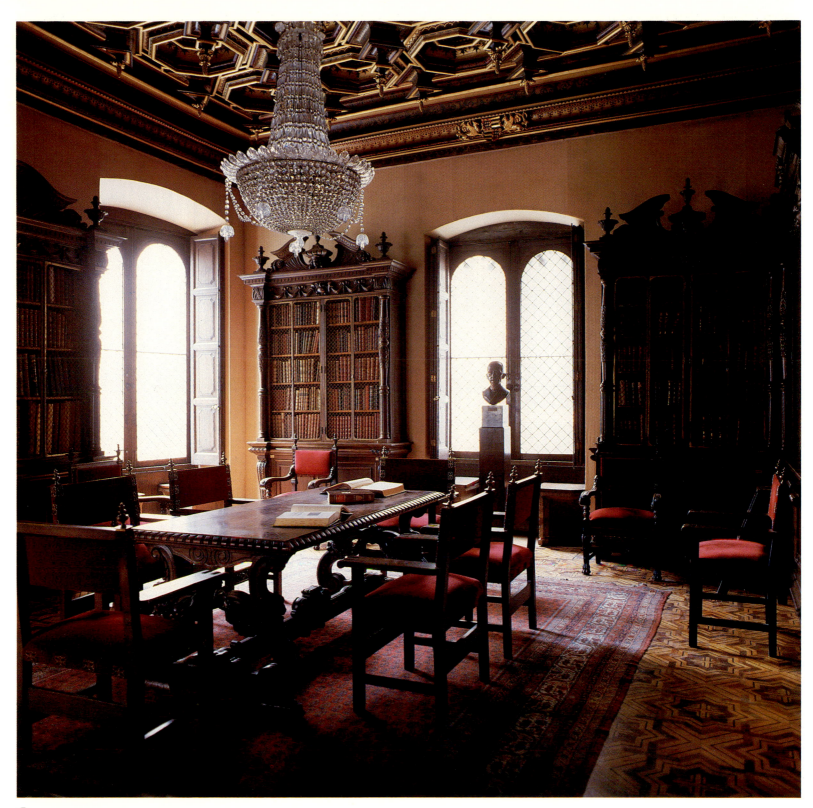

Casa de l'Ardiaca

Cloaked in silence, this library is situated in a Catalan Gothic building, dating from the twelfth and thirteenth centuries that has had close links with Barcelona's history since 1481 when King Fernando stayed in it. Although different architectural styles have left their mark, still visible are such elements as the magnificent ceiling seen here, and the beautiful inlay work of its wooden floors.

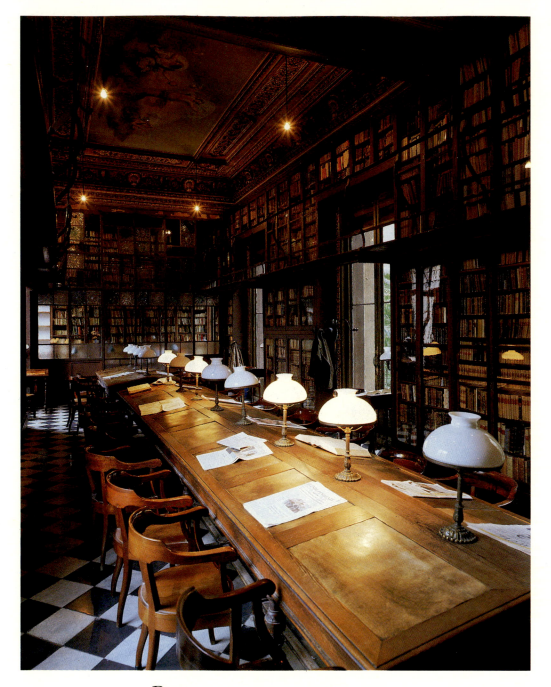

BIBLIOTECA DE L'ATENEU

Much fine Catalan poetry has been written and recited between these four walls since the foundation of the Ateneu Barcelonès as a cultural society in 1872. But the history of the building goes back much further. In 1796, the Baron de Sabassona planned the construction of a palace in the serene classical manner traditionally typical of Barcelona. All that remains today of that original building is the façade on the Carrer Canuda, the open staircase in the entrance hall, the romantic garden in the area behind, and the patrician first floor where the library is housed.

BIBLIOTECA DE CATALUNYA

The serenely beautiful Gothic arches of the old hospital of Santa Creu give the Library of Catalonia its special atmosphere, making it ideal for study, research or quiet thought. Founded in 1401 the hospital was built on the medieval model with two-storey bays round a rectangular cloister. It was restored by Adolf Florensa in 1968 for use as a library and is important as a cultural institution and, architecturally, as an exceptional example of Catalan Gothic.

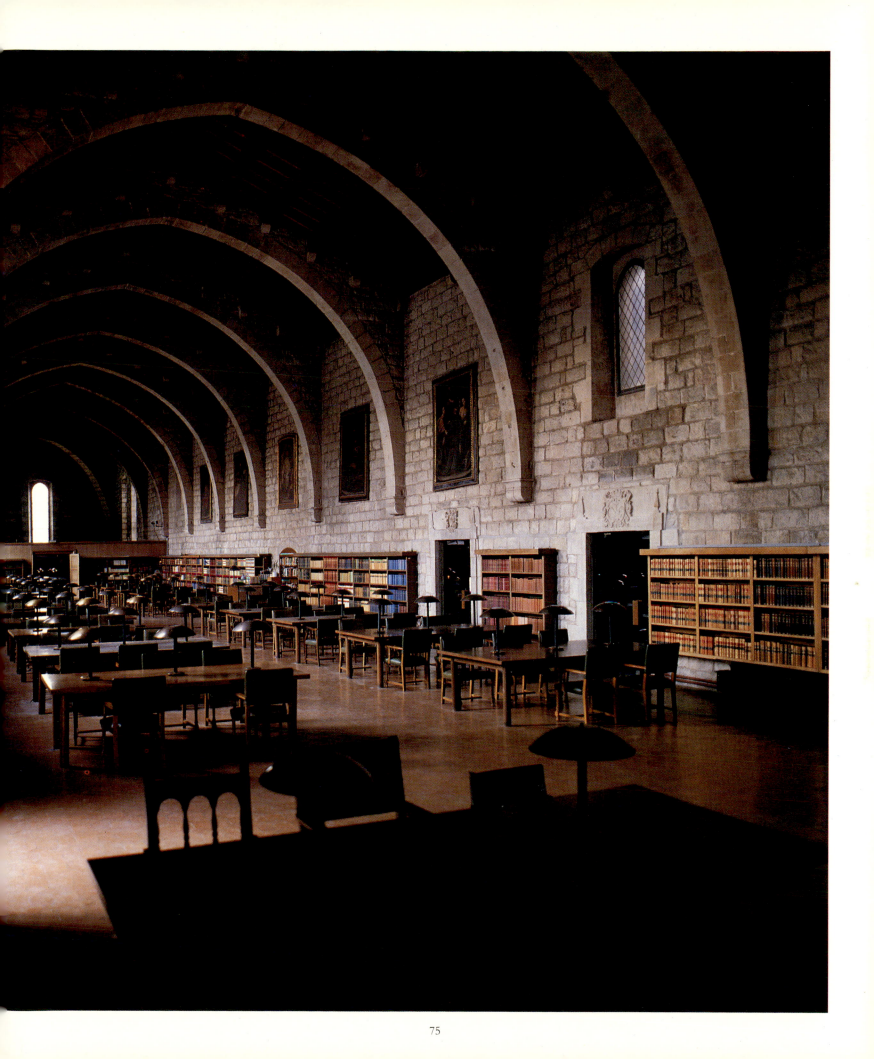

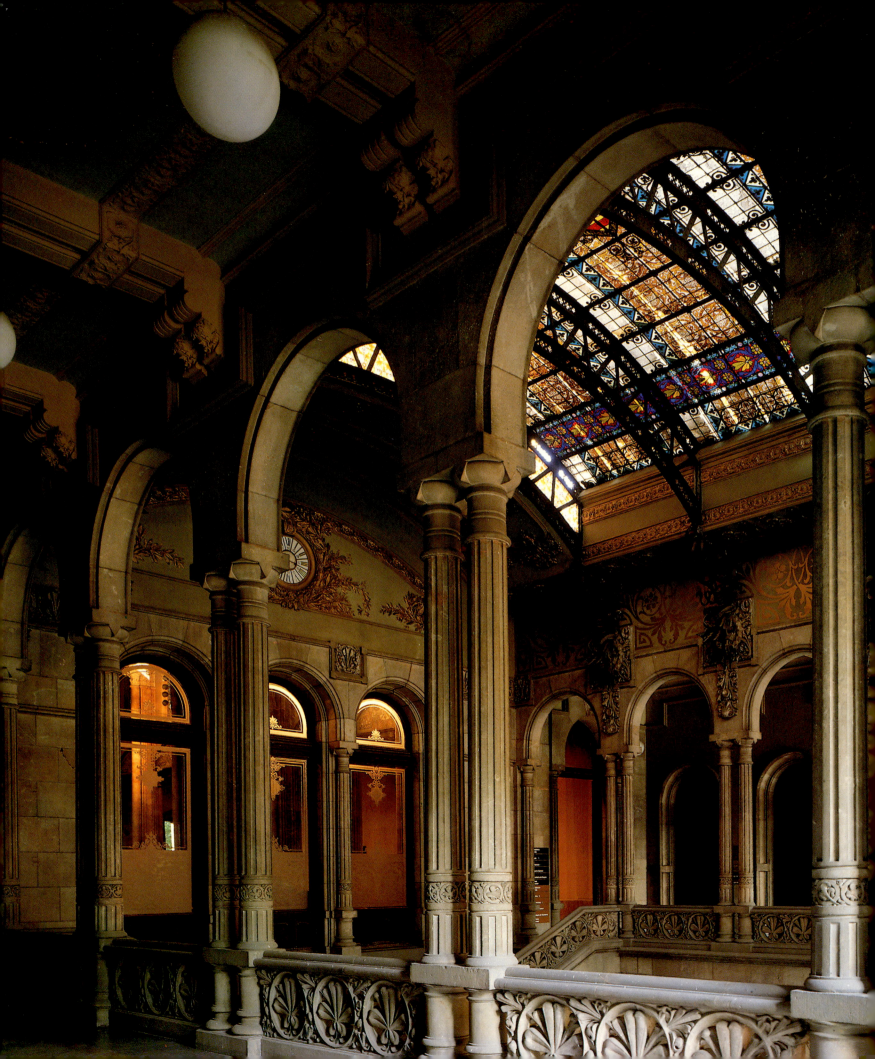

GOVERNMENT & CIVIC BUILDINGS

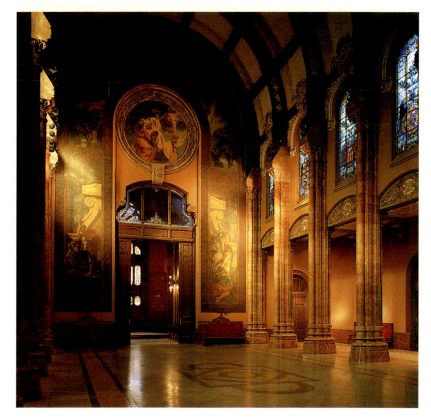

PALAU DE JUSTÍCIA

Ever concerned to marry different styles, the young Catalan architect Enric Sagnier i Villavechia combined a patrician Anglo-Saxon sense with an attempt at naturalism to give this important building its elegant and timeless character. Passages and corners in the interior are characteristic of Sagnier's work. The stone stairway carved with floral motifs meets, on the main floor, a series of stone arcades supporting the huge glass roof which lends an air of grandeur to the whole.

The stone columns beneath their delicate latticework of iron arches create an integrated setting for the richly imaginative interplay of positive and negative space where opaque and translucent materials meet in muted harmony, drawing the visitor inexorably on to the main hall.

GOVERN CIVIL

Count Roncali, when rebuilding the old Customs House which today houses the Govern Civil (Barcelona's local government), gave it a totally Neo-classical style, clearly influenced by the French aesthetic which is pervasive. There is something of the trompe-l'oeil in everything, both in the exterior stucco in imitation marble, and in the interior with its obvious air of qualité. Here the painted murals, the decorated ceiling, the gilding and moulding of the wood and plaster and the marble floors combine to convey the intended sense of superficial sumptuousness.

The great depth of field created by the corridors and intermediate spaces connecting the rooms generates a dialogue between materials, colours and forms which is emphasized by the natural light. Here the foot of a staircase becomes the protagonist of its surrounding space.

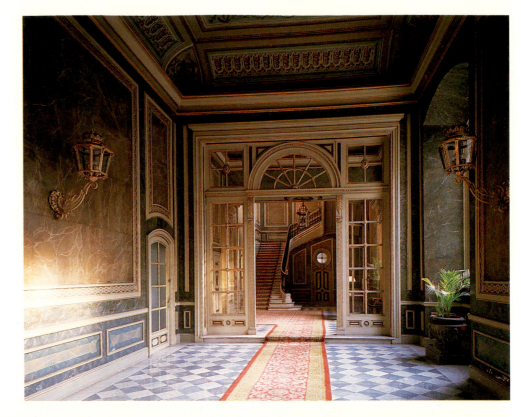

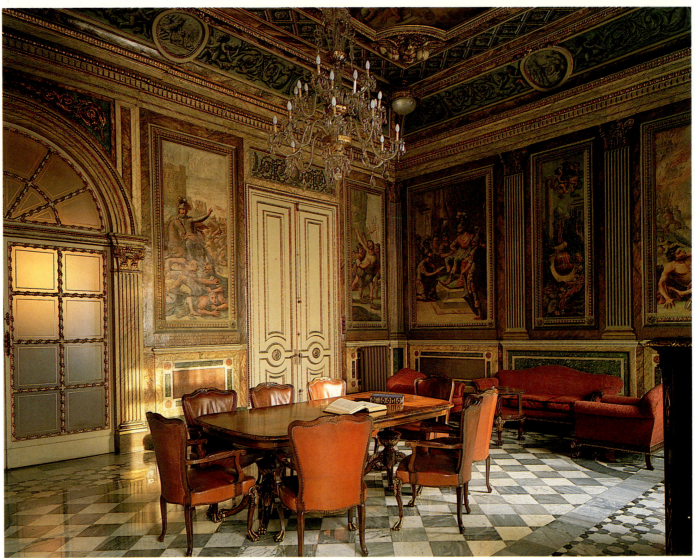

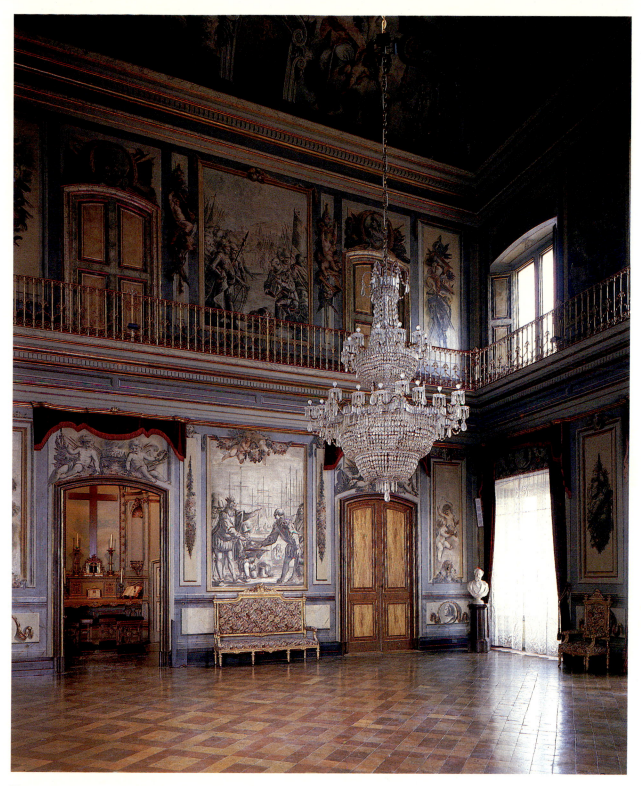

PALAU MOJA

Although constructed according to the most formal tenets of Neo-classicism between 1774 and 1786, the interior layout of the Palau Moja is rather confused. The original large garden has disappeared, leaving only a loggia. Successive fires damaged the palace until it was restored in 1984 to accommodate the offices of the Department of Culture of the Generalitat.

A large reception room and mural by 'El Vigatà' have survived but the recent renovation and restoration of the murals and original paint colours make it feel more like a museum than a room in regular use.

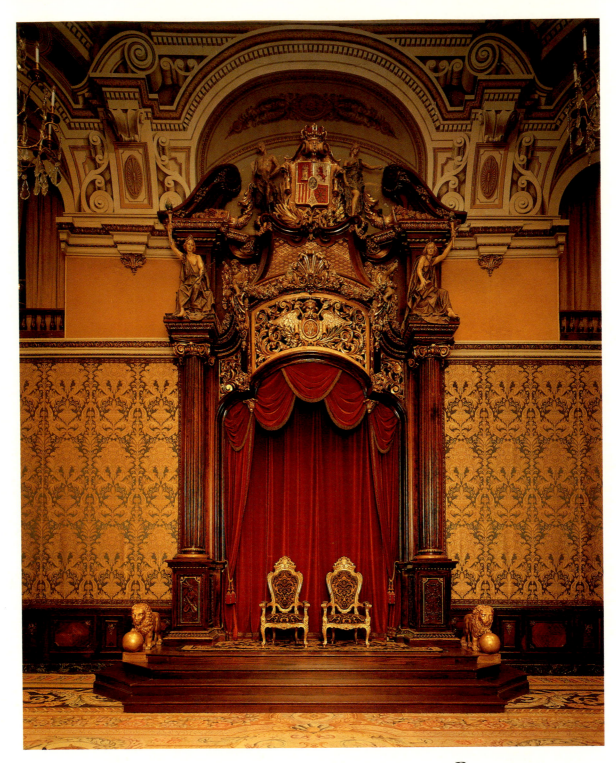

Palau de Pedralbes

Set in a luxuriant garden, this palace with its Neo-classical air and a hint of French in its decoration was the official residence of King Alfonso XIII. Official ceremonies took place in the throne room, with its remarkable canopy in polychrome wood depicting allegorically aspects of the life of royalty and the Spanish court. Today it is used for official receptions and other social events and in 1990 the Ceramics Museum was installed on the first floor.

Palau de la Generalitat de Catalunya, Saló de Sant Jordi

This peculiarly shaped hall was originally a chapel dedicated to Sant Jordi in which the area under the dome was occupied by the large altar. The paintings, carried out in 1926 by various artists, illustrate great moments from the history of Catalonia. The black virgin at the centre of the allegorical painting on the facing wall is Catalonia's patroness, 'La Moreneta'. Note too the remarkably fine glass chandelier that occupies the centre of the room.

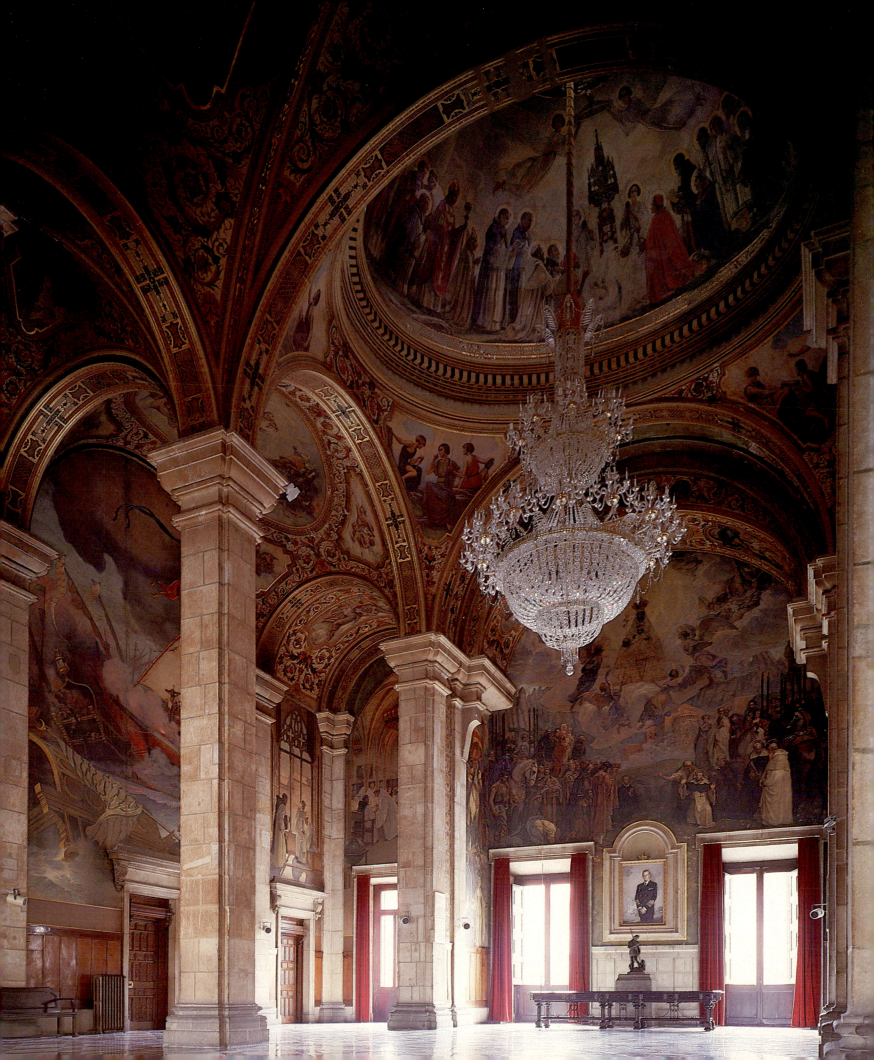

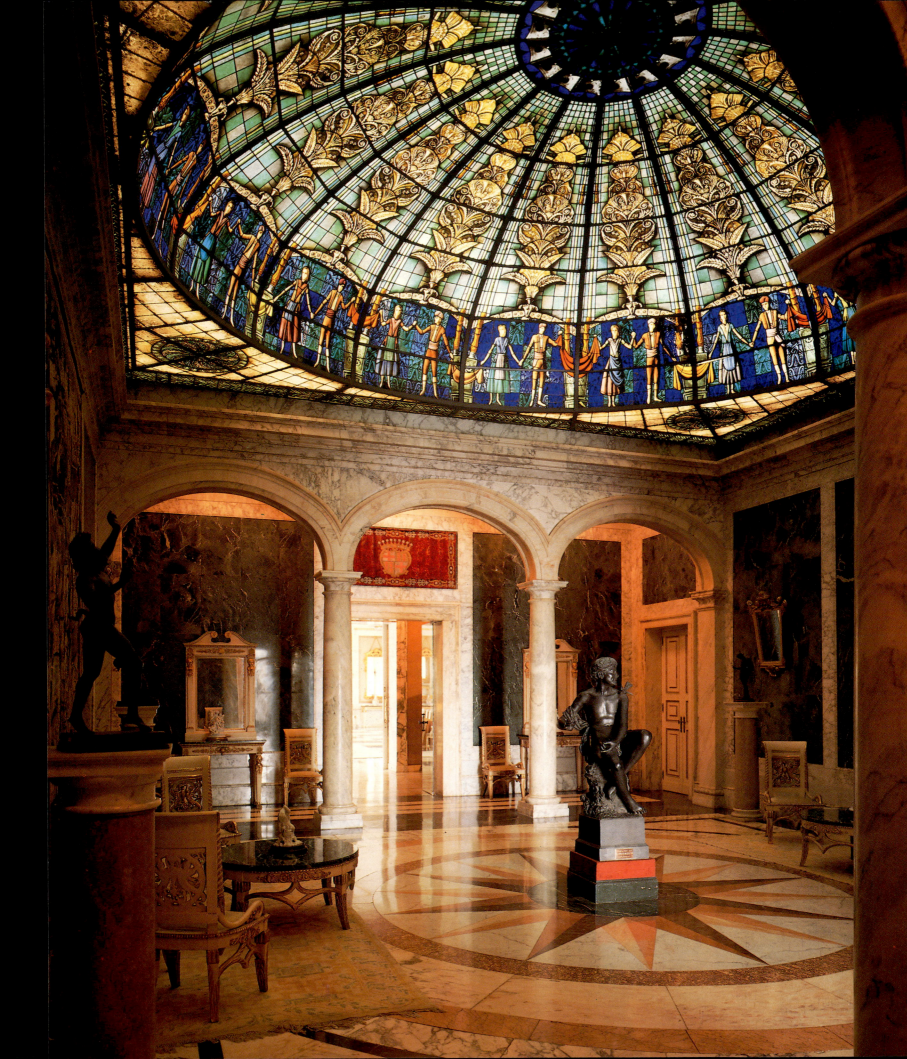

Palauet Albèniz

At the entrance to the official residence in Barcelona of the King and Queen of Spain, this dome, painted by Salvador Dalí, welcomes the illustrious guests with the blue of the Mediterranean and the sky in Cadaques. Despite the apparent banality and prosaic quality of the official receptions held here, these luxurious rooms have been privy to many decisive conversations, infinitely reflected by the mirrors, and discreetly locked away when finished like valuable treasures.

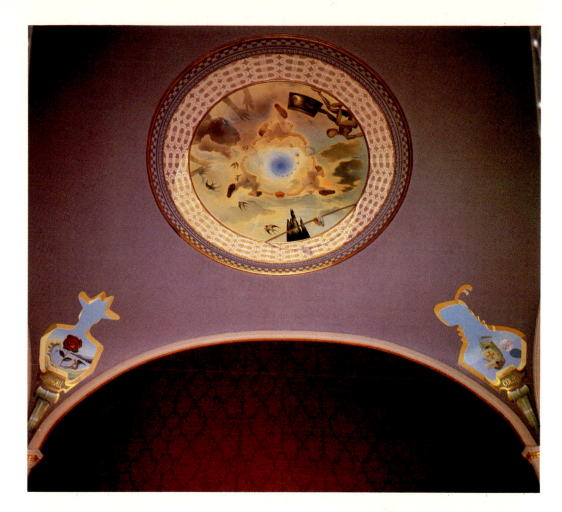

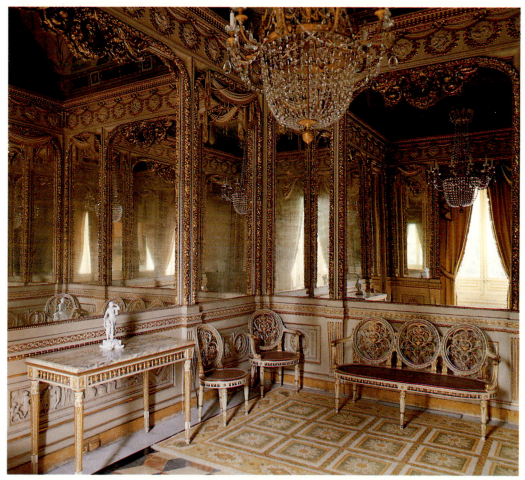

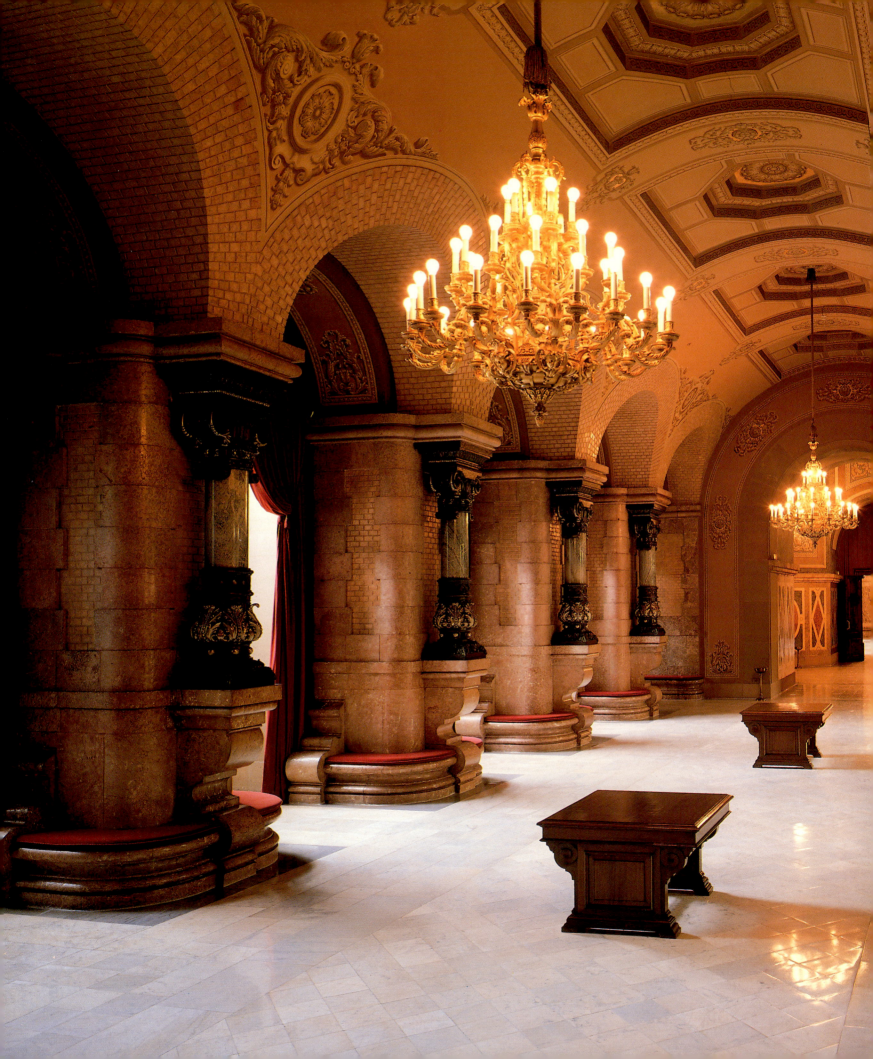

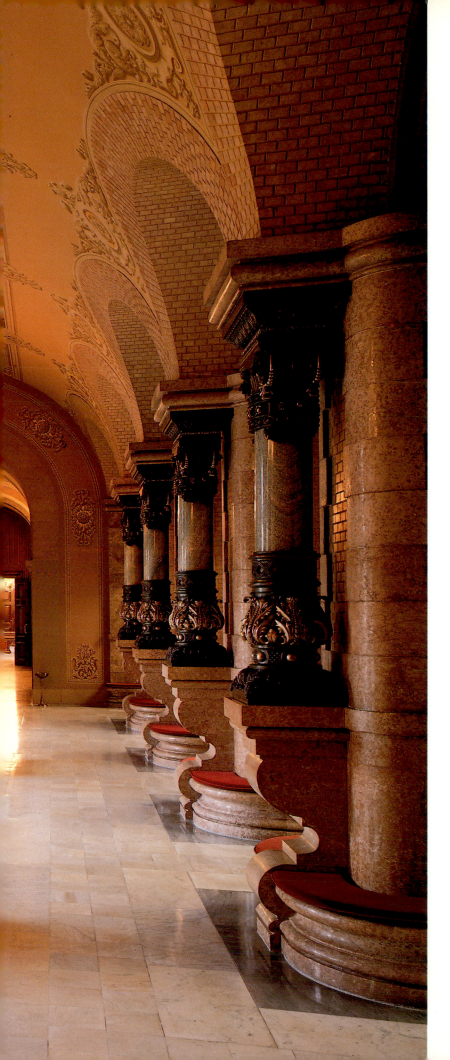

Parlament de Catalunya

This magnificent old corridor, still called 'els pasos perduts' (the lost steps) could speak volumes about the vicissitudes of the Catalan people and their laws. What was formerly part of the fortress (La Ciutadella), then a royal residence converted on the accession of the Bourbons in 1899, is now the seat of the Catalan government. The parade ground was transformed into a fine garden by the great French landscape designer Forestier.

DIPÒSIT DE LES AIGÜES

It was the young Gaudí, when assistant to the architect Josep Fontseré i Mestres, who calculated the structure of this building for the town's water supply. As a result his teachers exempted him from attending classes and passed him in 'Strength of Materials' without his taking the exam. The unique building, in exposed brick, is simply a large hypostyle supporting an enormous uncovered water cistern. Restored in 1988, it is now an exhibition centre for the COOB (Barcelona Olympics Organization Committee).

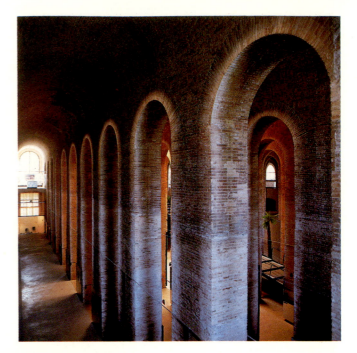

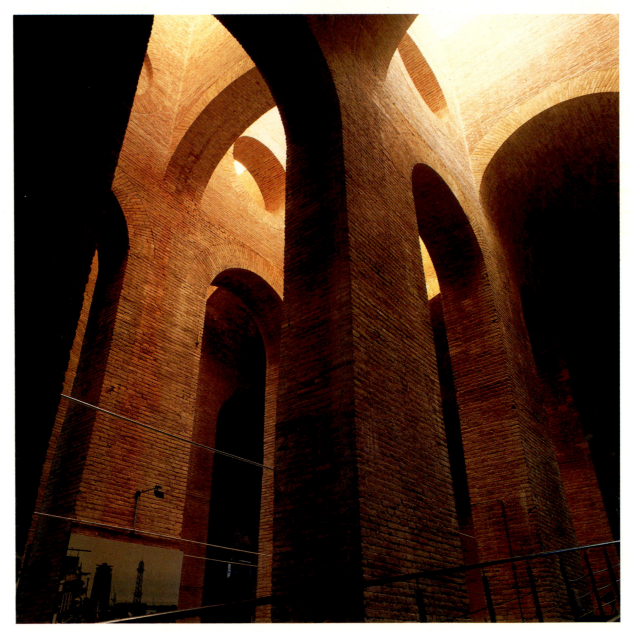

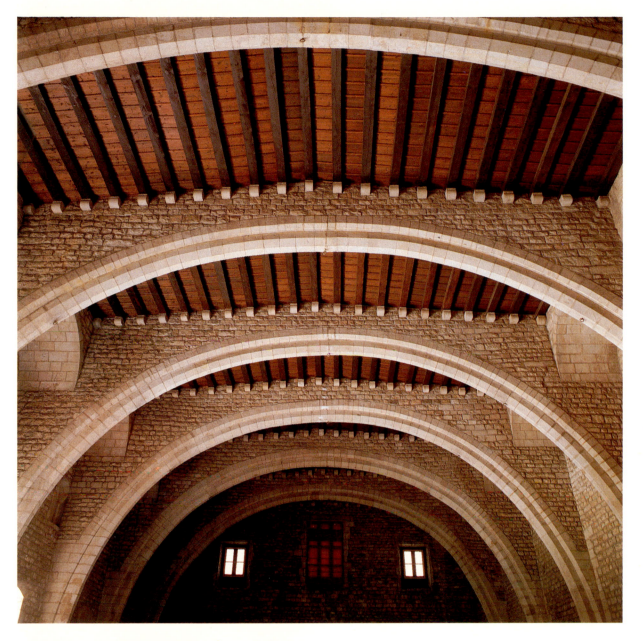

PALAU REIAL MAJOR

This ancient palace dates from the tenth century or earlier. A transformation between 1359 and 1370, by Guillem Carbonell to a commission from Pere III, resulted in the great hall or 'chamber of adornments,' later called the Tinell salon. The old wooden ceiling rests on six diaphragmatic round arches. Years after the Caspe Treaty (1412), Fernando and Isabel are said to have stayed here, as is Christopher Columbus bringing tales of that New World which, paradoxically, was for many years denied to the Catalan people, always better traders than conquerors.

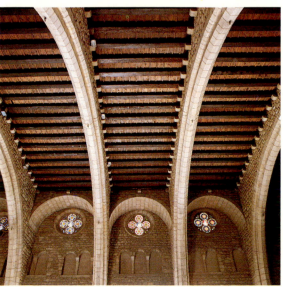

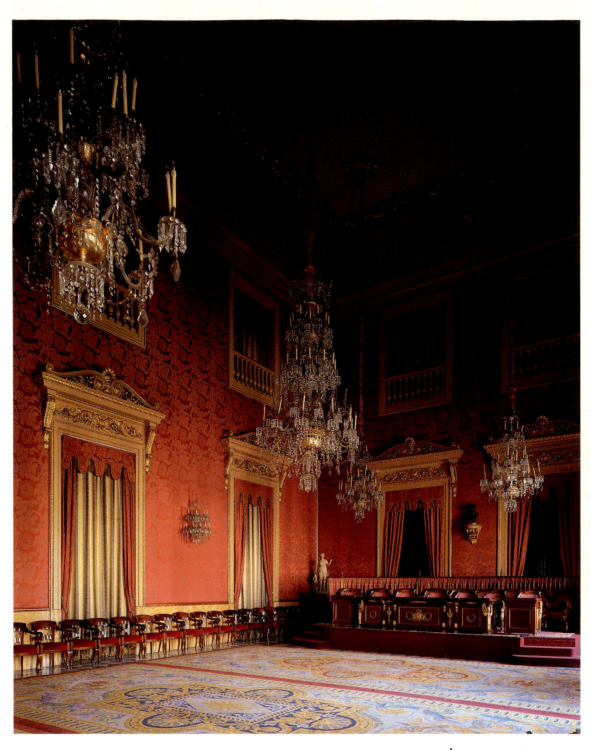

SALÓ DAURAT DE LLOTJA

One of the purest and most famous examples of Neo-classicism in Barcelona is to be found on the first floor of the old Stock Exchange. Reached by the staircase of honour with its fine balustrade, the Saló Daurat was decorated at the end of the eighteenth century. Furniture, tapestries and paintings are all original. With its superb decoration and glittering chandeliers it is a truly brilliant setting for formal occasions. Today the Saló Daurat is used for such important cultural events as the admission of a new member to the Royal Academy of Fine Arts.

AJUNTAMENT DE BARCELONA, SALÓ DE CENT

Since 1372 this building has undergone many changes in its long life at the heart of Barcelona's municipal life, and is a credit to the democratic skills of the Catalan people. Catalan Gothic in style, with the addition of atypical Near Eastern elements, successive changes and restoration have not been able to damage its aesthetic qualities or its character as a political forum. The clean-cut arches, and columns with double capitals, the rose-tinted windows and polychromatic carvings decorated with gold leaf are all inspirational features.

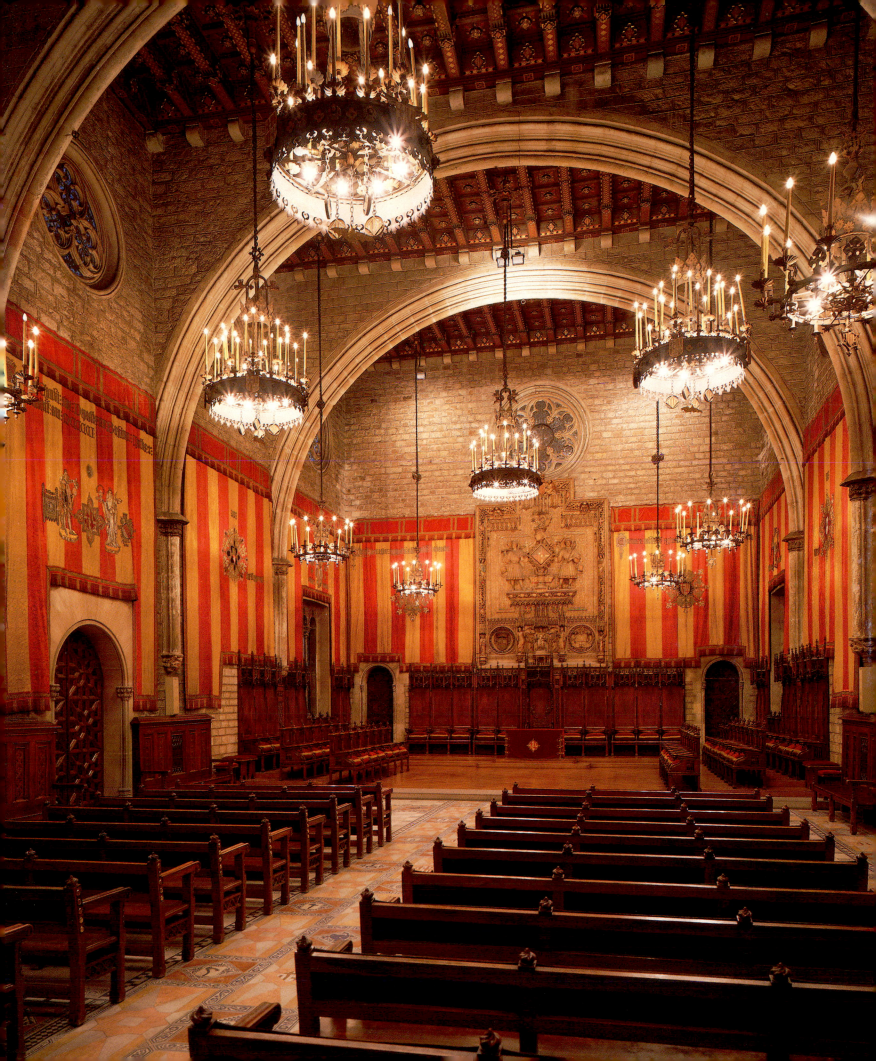

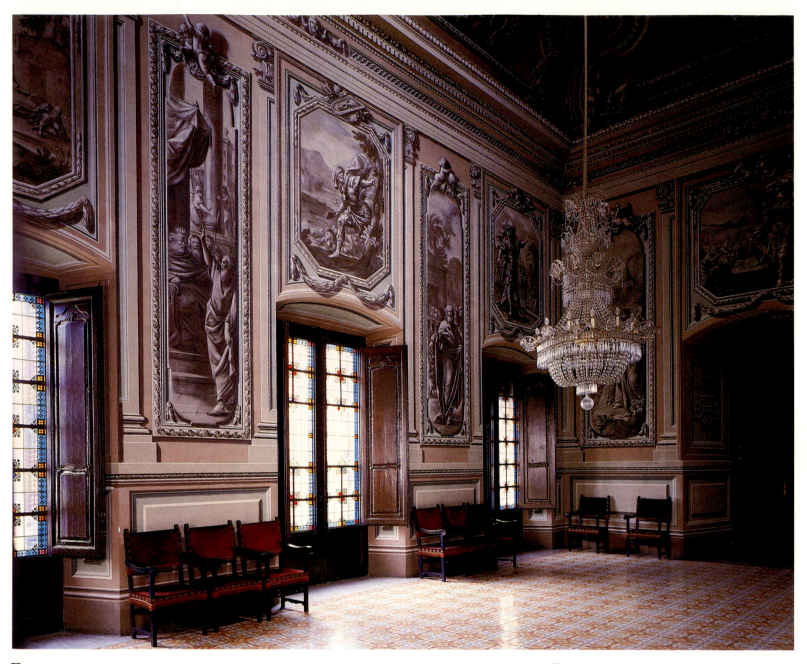

PALAU EPISCOPAL

Abutting the Roman wall at the Porta Bisbal and opening on to Bisbe, the Bishops' Palace, the seat of the bishops of Barcelona since the twelfth century, encapsulates the city's entire architectural history. Over the centuries it has undergone numerous restorations and extensions. In the large ceremonial room hang the well-known grey-toned paintings by the late-Baroque artist Francesc Pla, known as 'El Vigata'.

DELEGACIÓ DEL GOVERN A CATALUNYA

This entrance hall in the Palau Montaner is a fine example of that superb collaboration between architects, sculptors, glaziers and other craftsmen which was one of the hallmarks of Catalan Modernisme. *The harmoniously proportioned imperial staircase is set in a courtyard tiled with floral motifs just as if a carpet had been placed there in the centre. The walls are decorated with richly painted murals, and the ceilings with typical* modernista *motifs. The roof is made of glass in the form of a continuous cannonade arch, one of the most clearly defined and balanced elements of the entire building.*

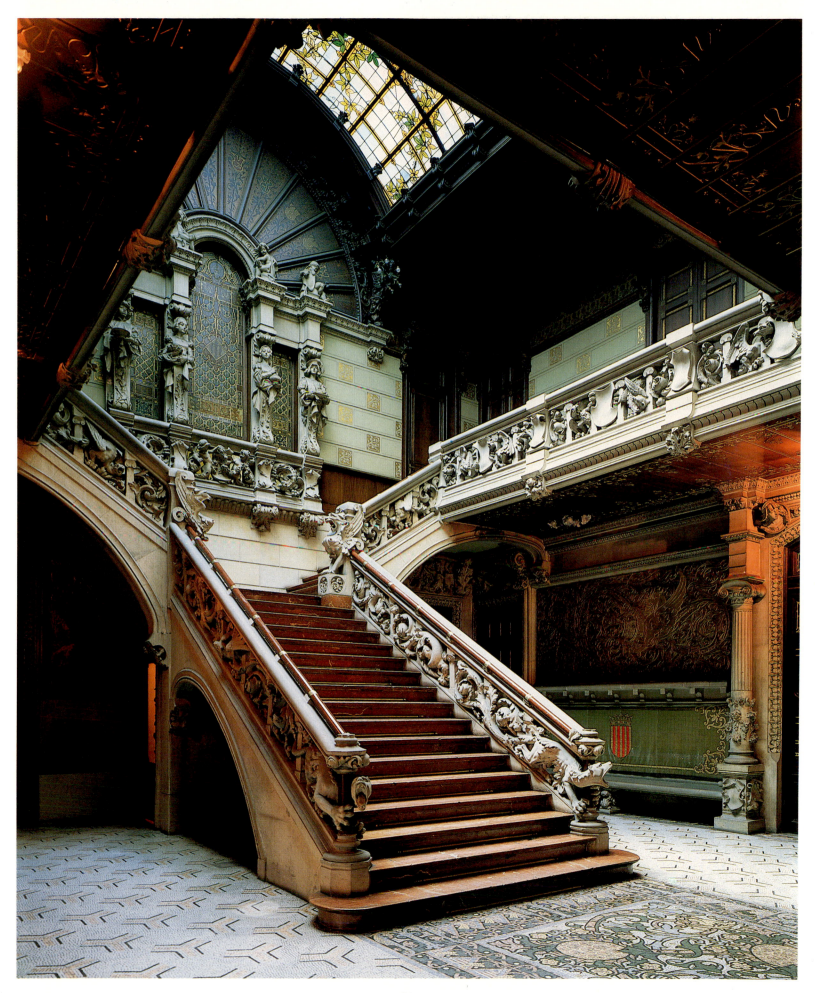

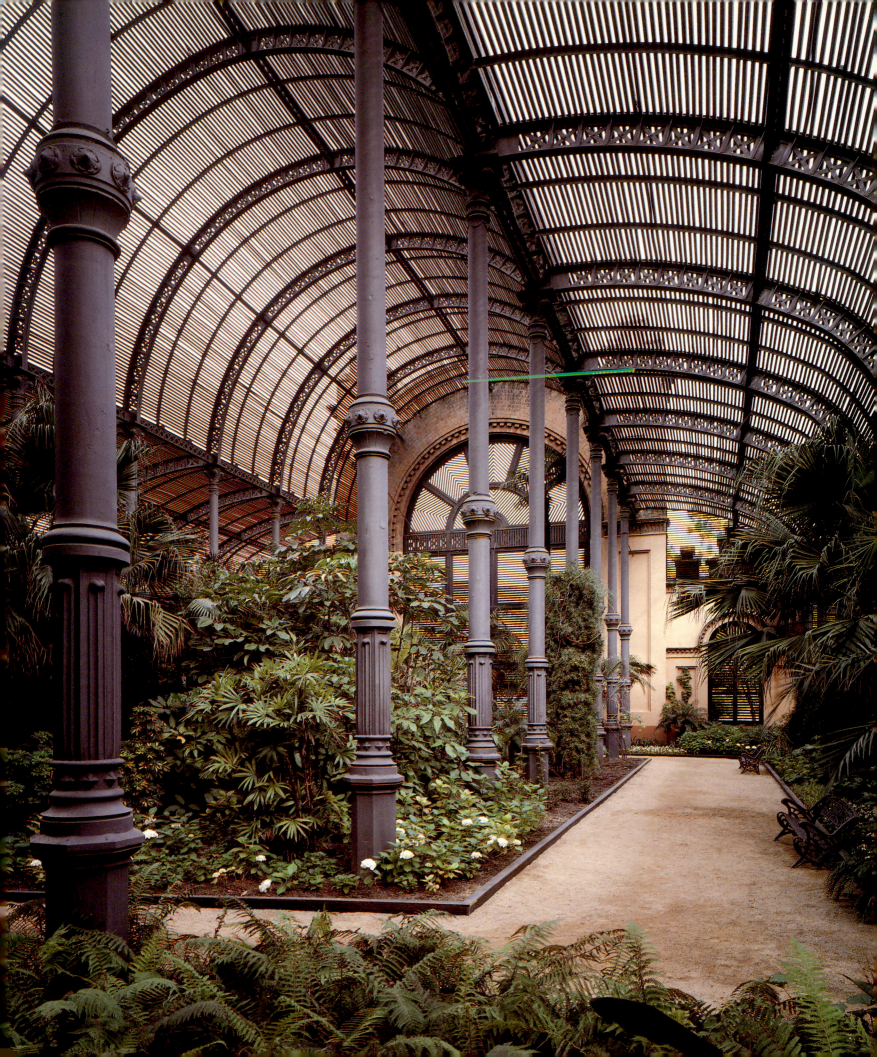

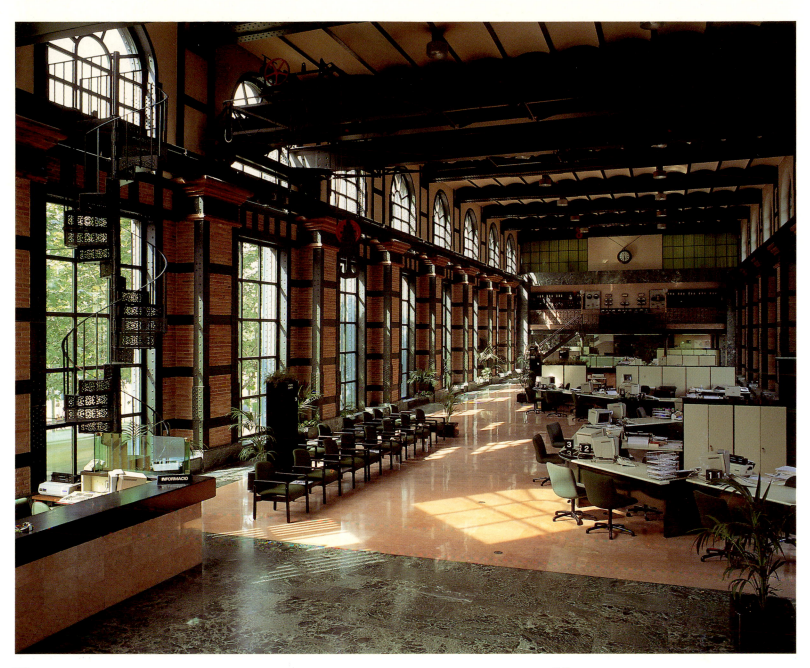

UMBRACLE

Standing in the Parc de la Ciutadella, this glasshouse was built by Josep Fontserè i Mestres in 1884. Constructed from cast-iron columns, bent metal wires and wooden sheets, the Umbracle has a very interesting lobed section which distinguishes it from the neighbouring structures: the Hivernacle and the Geology and Zoology Museum. In 1886, Jaume Gustà reshaped it for use as a ballroom and conference hall, but today it is once more put to its original use.

HIDROELÈCTRICA DE CATALUNYA

The Catalan Electricity Centre was founded in 1896, a descendant of the Catalan Gas Lighting Company. Flaqués i Urpi's project was inspired by modern German engineering. The building is made up of elongated parallel bays, which used to contain the machine room and steam generators. The conversion of the building transformed the old machine room into offices, at the far end of which is the magnificently restored original control panel of the old heating centre. It is worth coming here to pay the electricity bill, as our grandparents used to do.

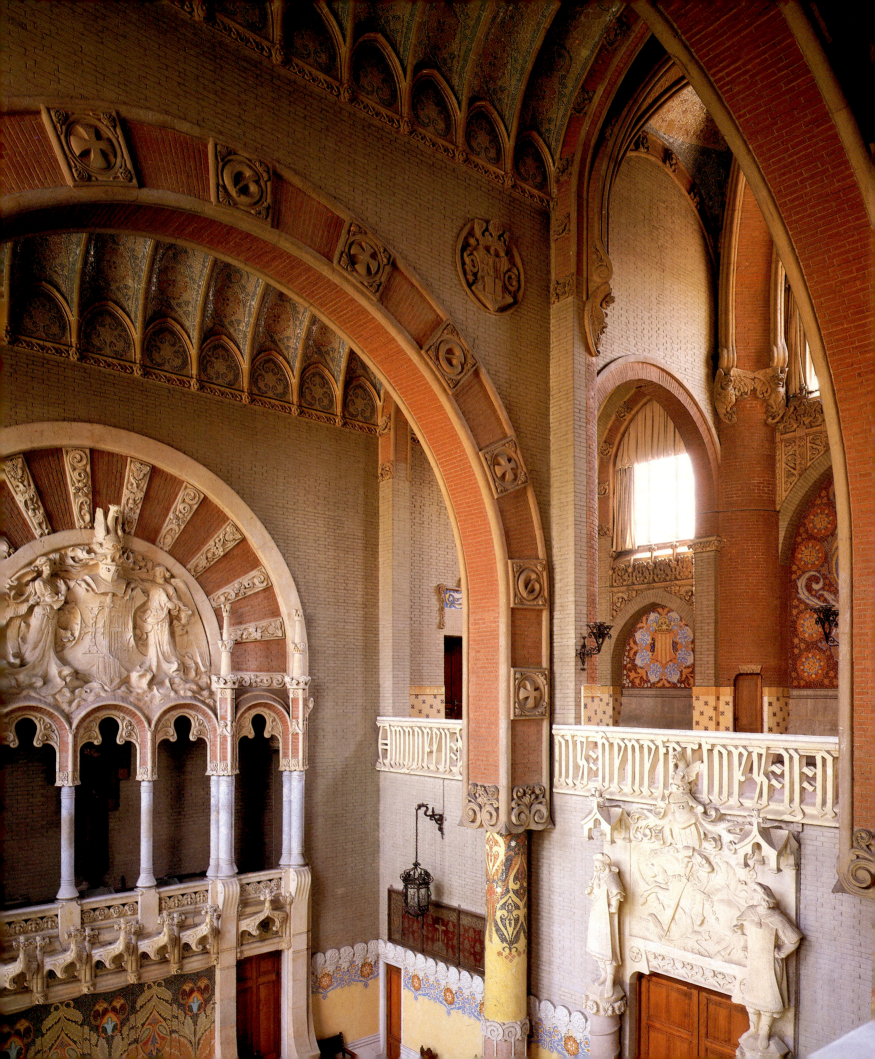

HOSPITALS
& RESIDENCES

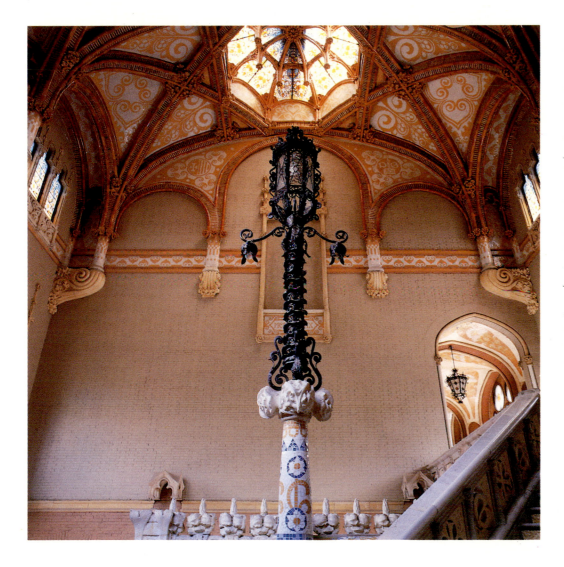

HOSPITAL DE LA SANTA CREU I SANT PAU

The construction of this large model hospital in the early years of this century, under the terms of the will of Pau Gil i Serra, was of such magnitude that it needed contributions from the Hospital de la Santa Creu, from the public and from the city of Barcelona to complete it. The hospital was to be called St Paul's and the architect was Lluís Domènech i Montaner. Forty-eight pavilions, a church and offices set in an enormous garden are wisely connected by convenient underground passages. As with all modernista *buildings the collaboration between architects, artists and craftsmen was an essential feature. In this respect the works of the sculptor Pablo Gargallo are of particular interest here. As in this staircase, the combination of stone, iron and ceramics sets up an interplay of materials and forms both indicative of the architectural space and cleverly integrated with it.*

CLÍNICA BARRAQUER

Built on the eve of the Civil War in 1936, the Barraquer Clinic quickly became a world-famous centre for ophthalmology. The building includes Expressionist elements with touches from the Academicist tradition. Partially restored, the interiors keep the expressive appearance of high-tech Modernisme, with rather an Art Deco feel. For years, people of all races came in with the hope of having their sight restored. When that miracle was achieved, they could walk out on to the Av. de Muntaner, a long festive avenue which loses itself in greenery on its way down to the sea.

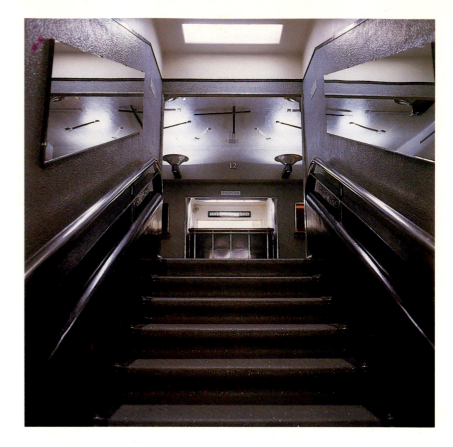

CONSELLERIA DE SANITAT DE LA GENERALITAT DE CATALUNYA

The present headquarters of the Department of Health was built at the turn of the century by Camil Oliveras i Gensana. Its modernista decoration conceals an incipient rationalism. The typically Mediterranean brickwork and the magnificent earth-tone stuccos, illuminated by the light filtering through the skylight, provide an expertly modernista atmosphere, which it is our duty to preserve and pass on.

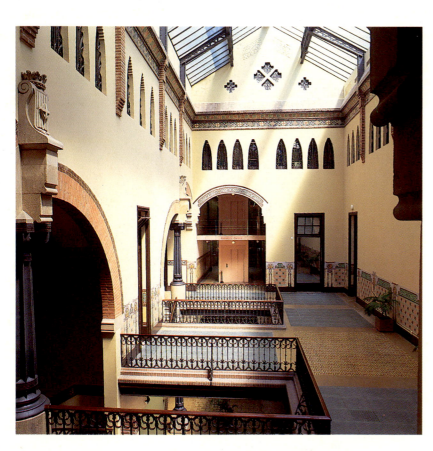

RESIDÈNCIA FRANCESC LAYRET

Behind its exceptional façade, this large and singularly enchanting house conceals some of Barcelona's most impressive and least visited interiors. The large courtyard around which the entire building is constructed serves as an entrance hall leading to the various rooms. Up above, the balcony overlooking the central space represents a remarkable coalescence of craftsmanship. The visitor to what is now a retirement home is greeted at the door by a calm and elegant beauty

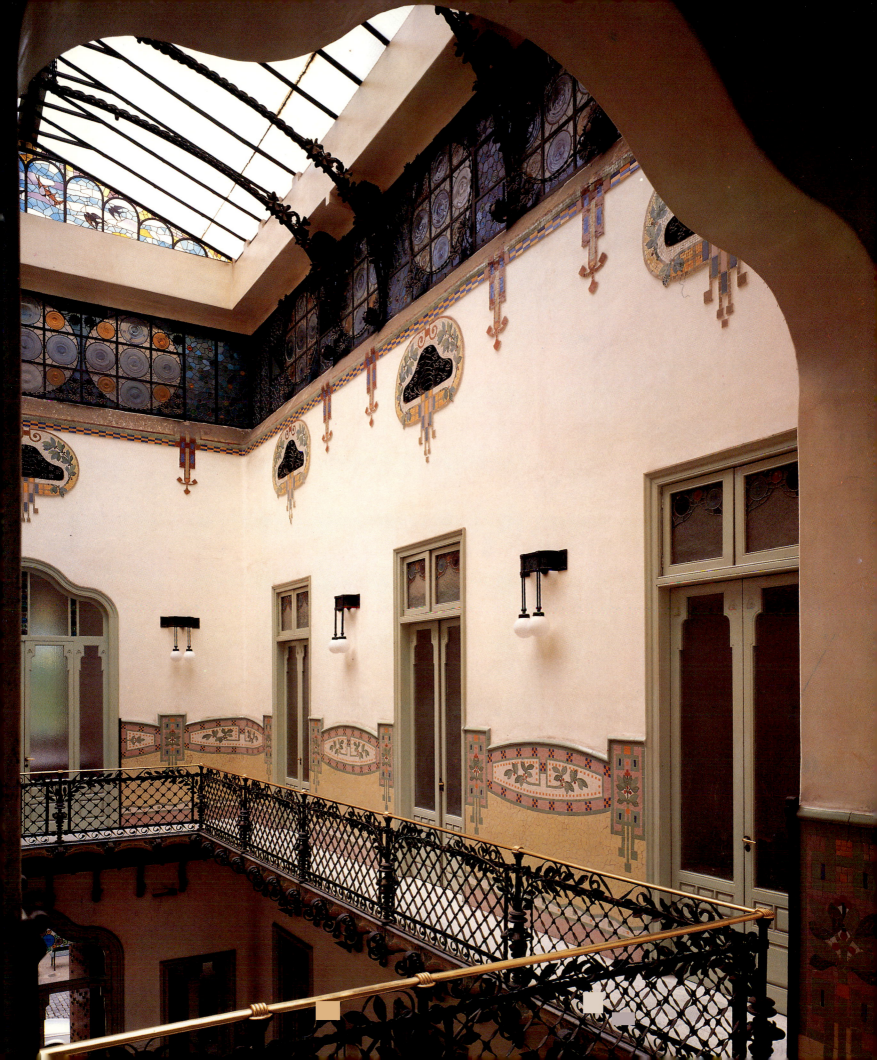

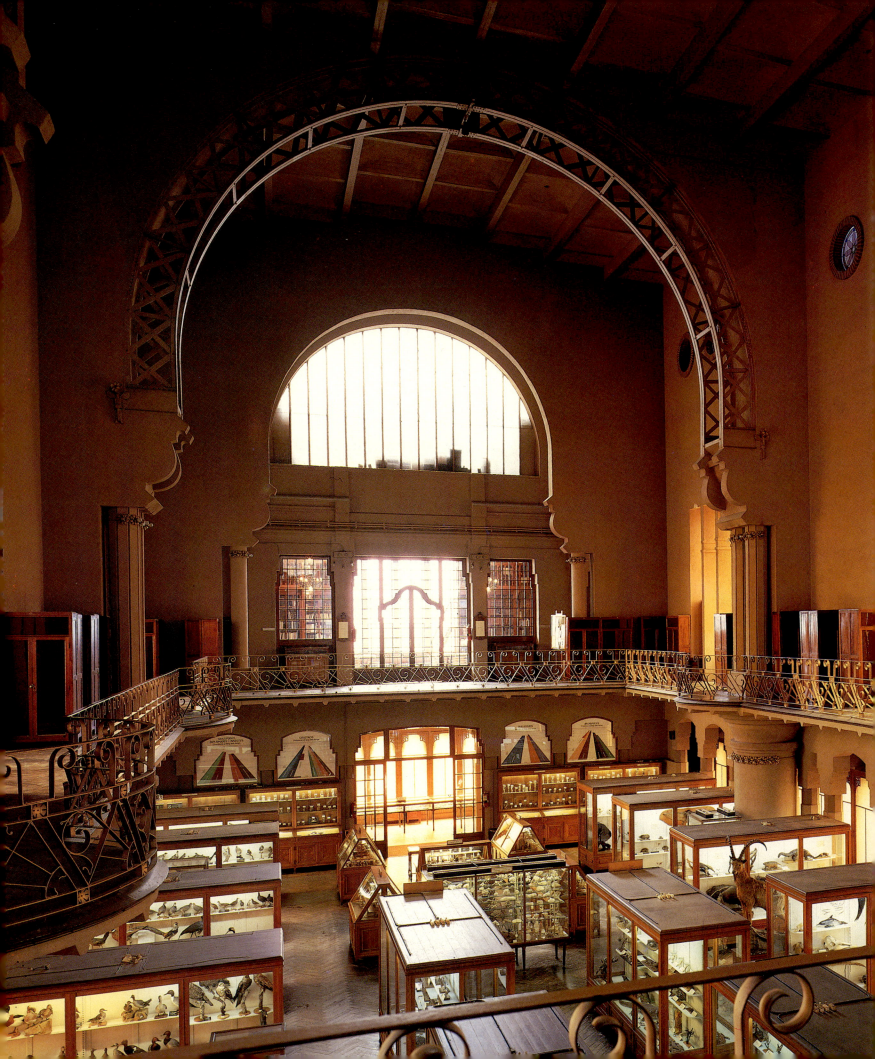

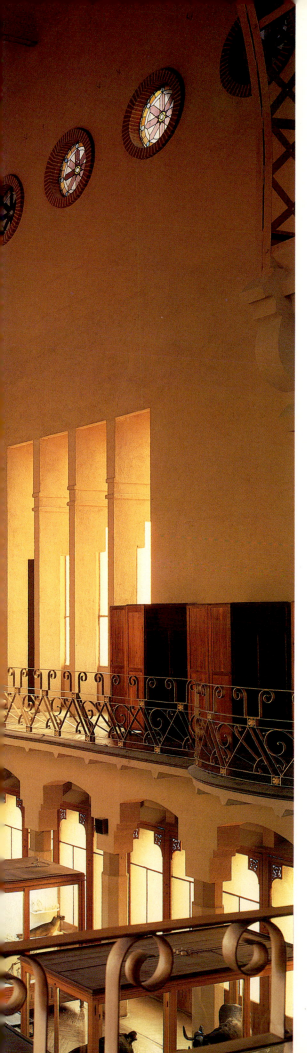

MUSEUMS

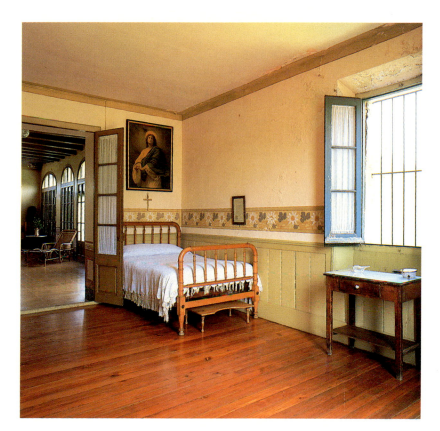

MUSEU DE ZOOLOGIA

The great 1888 Universal Exhibition was the cue for the construction of a large number of new buildings, one of which was this magnificent 'Castle of the Three Dragons' situated in the Ciutadella Park. Designed as a restaurant by Domènech i Montaner in his characteristic style, it never functioned as such since the building work was not finished until after the end of the Exhibition. For many years it has housed the Zoology Museum, which has recently been carefully restored.

MUSEU VERDAGUER

The renaissance in Catalan literature would have been inconceivable without the eminent figure of Mossèn Cinto Verdaguer. Here, in this house turned museum, once a country house known as Vil.la Joana, the great poet spent the last days of his life. In 1977, the centenary of his great poem 'L'Atlàntida', more rooms were opened which have made the old house a place of poetic pilgrimage, a temple to Catalonian culture, full of the poet's books and manuscripts, of portraits and of photographs.

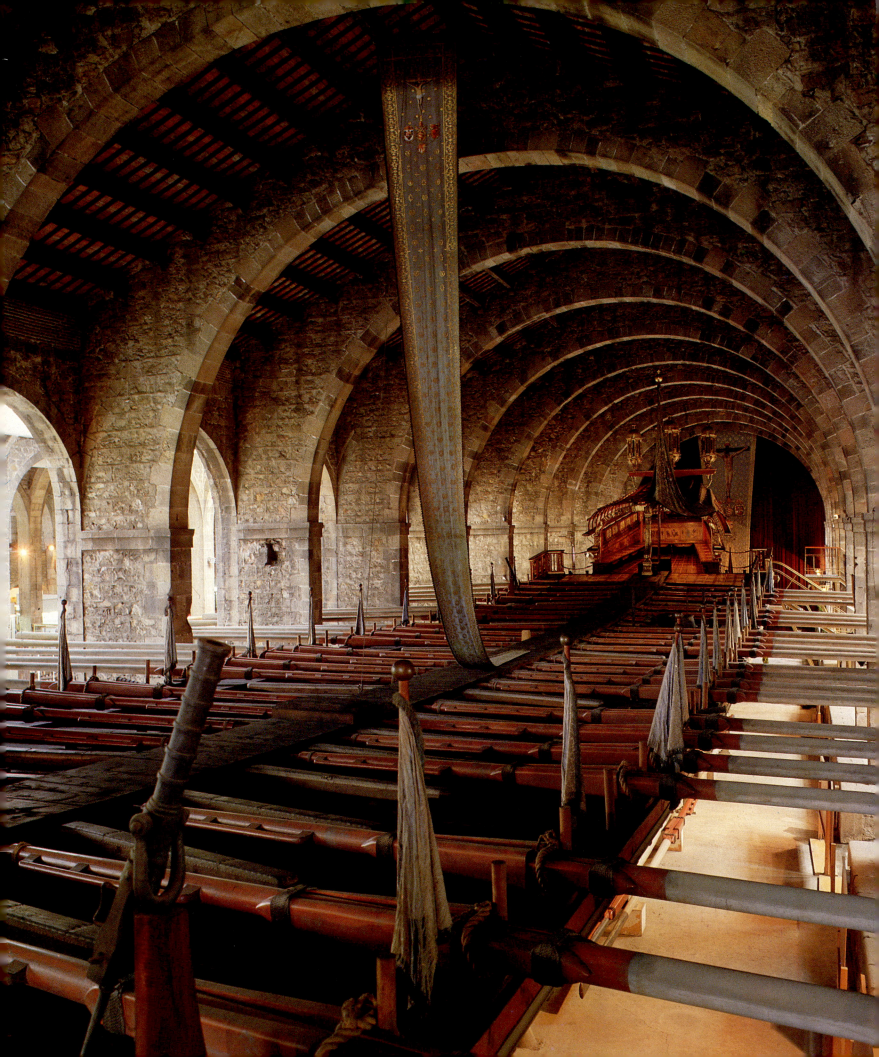

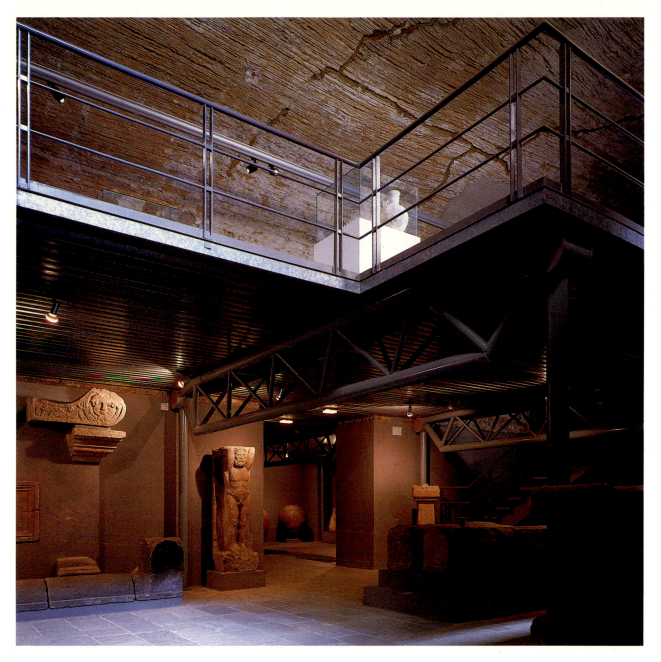

Reials drassanes

When the city was closed off behind Roman walls ships were built on the beach. But expansion into the Mediterranean under Pere III meant the construction of a shipyard where dozens of galleys could be built. The shipyard's architects contrived a system of apparently longitudinal bays (which were in fact subdivided by round arches) designed to cover large areas. Then, until the creation of the Maritime Museum, the building suffered a long period of disuse and fell into disrepair. Today, figureheads, nautical and astronomical equipment and a replica of Columbus's caravel all attest to the past splendours of Barcelona's maritime history.

Museu d'història de la ciutat

Between 1497 and 1515 Joan Hostalrich and his wife, Joana de Montbui had built for themselves a house befitting the nobility. Called Casa Padellàs it was typically Catalan Gothic in layout though its iconographic detail and decoration borrows more from the Renaissance. The opening of the new Via Laietana in the 1920s saw the house transferred stone by stone to the corner of the Plaça del Rei where, beneath the foundations, was found a fourth-century Roman city extending under the whole square and the Palau Major. Recent restoration has made it easier to see each historic period more clearly.

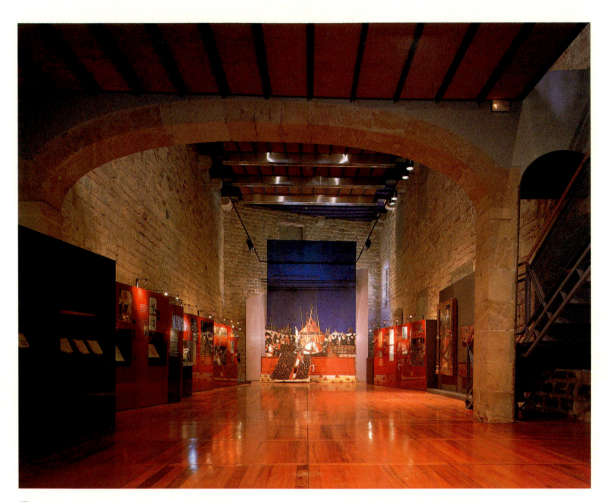

PIA ALMOINA

Constructed in 1423 to house the Pia Almoina, one of the oldest charitable foundations in Europe (1009), this singular building, typical of the late Middle Ages in atmosphere, draws together the magnificent architectural complex which includes the cathedral. What sheer pleasure it is to stroll across the square to the sound of bells and the fluttering of pigeons to enter this old-new space. Once one of Barcelona's main hospitals, since renovated, the old building is now the Diocesan Museum and full of exquisite religious works of art from all periods. As a museum it is a fine example of that difficult achievement of a delicate balance between historical and architectural rigour and the use of new materials and colours, the key to understanding Catalonia's amazing architectural past with a contemporary vision.

MUSEU DE LA MÚSICA

In this entrance hall a sophisticated and complex use of materials - tessellated flooring, columns with sculpted bases and floral capitals, a stone fountain - all seem to pay homage to a foreshortened stone staircase which deftly conceals its modest dimensions so that the whole conveys a magical sense of equilibrium characteristic of Puig i Cadafalch's other great designs. While on the one hand the main façade is one of his classic reinterpretations of the Gothic, the back of the building is bare of the sculptures and Gothic features typical of the period. However, the heterogeneity of the interior was not a barrier to installing the Museum of Music here in 1980.

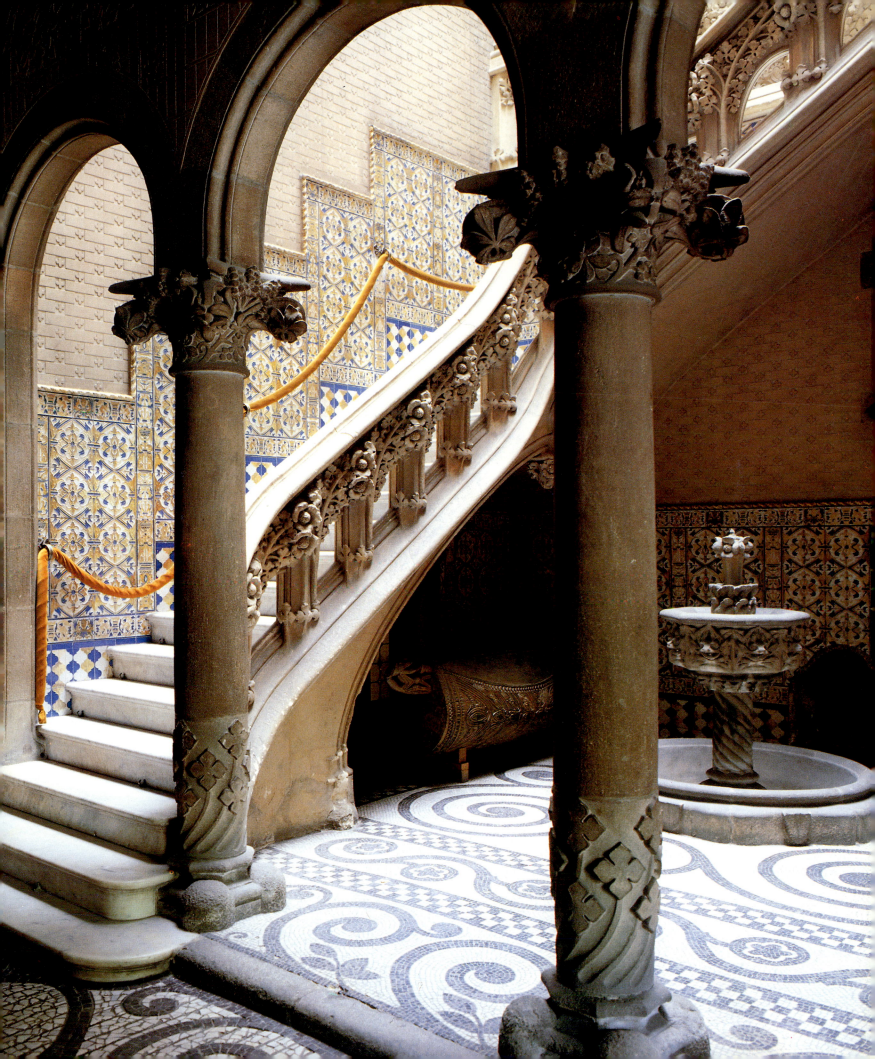

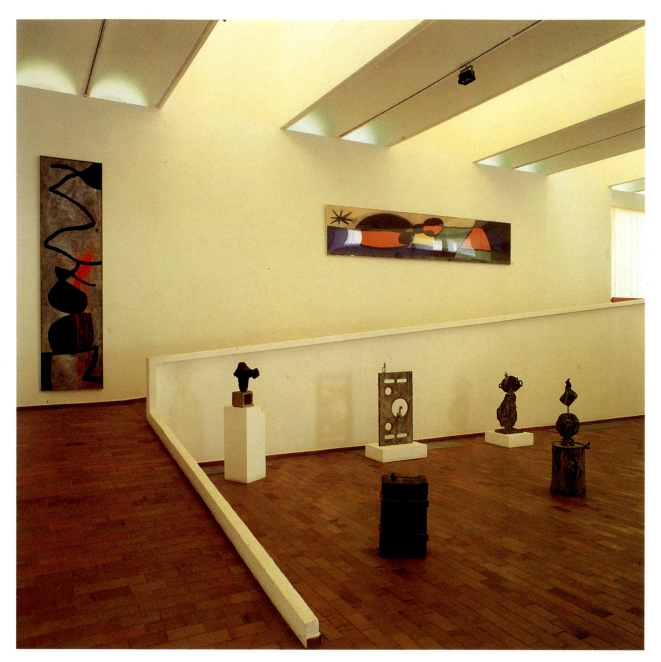

Fundació Joan Miró

Not a hint of Stendhal's 'museum illness' will be found in this building, a gem by Sert which confirms Barcelona's avant-garde status. Strong filtered light allows the visitor to view works of art without any sense of claustrophobia; the terrace seen here is a unique sculptural space.

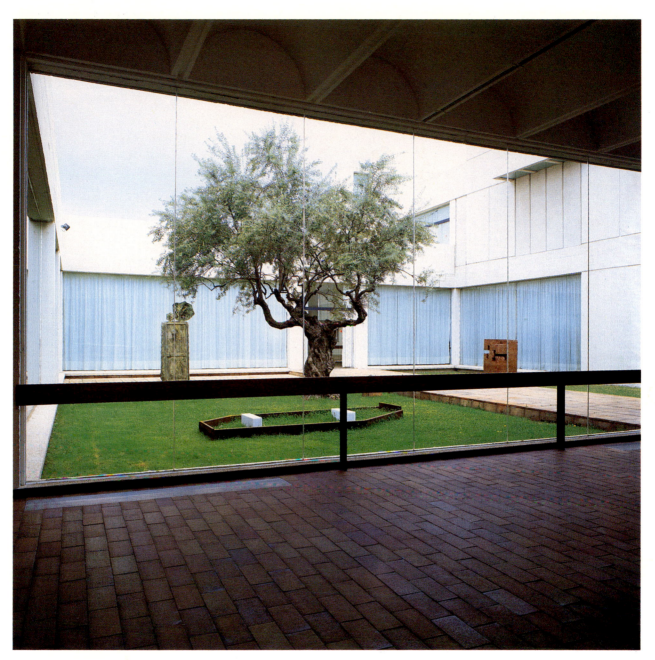

The Fundació Joan Miró, with its wonderful view of the city, was opened in 1979 to house an important Miró collection and to hold regular contemporary art exhibitions. Designed by Josep Lluis Sert, it displays a masterful use of space within the total environment. Here the poetic movement of Calder's work is set against a background of rigid concrete.

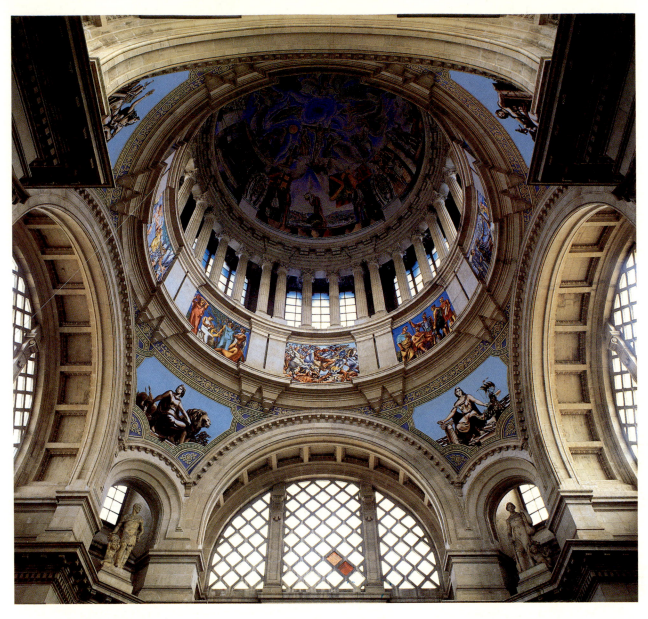

MUSEU D'ART DE CATALUNYA

*If Puig i Cadafalch's general plan had been
carried out by the time of the 1929
International Exhibition Catalan architecture
and more specifically* Modernisme *would have
received the universal acknowledgement it
deserved. What prevented this was the imposition
of a style - the synthesis of several illustrious
styles of Spanish architecture - which, though of
evident strength, was far from being a true
expression of Barcelona's cultural spirit. The
National Palace, showpiece of this architectural
ensemble and designed as a residence for the
Kings of Spain, now houses the Museum of Art
containing probably the finest Romanesque art
collection in the world. Grandiloquent and of
special architectonic value, this building appears
to pay no heed to classical rules. There are well-
conceived sequences, however: the double staircase,
the monumental oval hall and the stylized dome
to which the Francesc Galí paintings form a
perfect complement.*

MUSEU TEXTIL I DE LA INDUMENTÀRIA

*This is one of the Gothic pearls of the Carrer
Montcada near the Museu Picasso. The original
construction dates from the fourteenth century
and the building retains a good part of the
original structure. Doors and windows typical of
the Renaissance were added in the sixteenth
century. In the eighteenth century, the Marquès
de Lió rebuilt it completely, though respecting the
physiognomy of the courtyard so as to preserve
the building's profound Gothic spirit.
More work in 1969 highlighted the beautiful
work seen here, executed in wood and fine gold,
once a communicating window between two halls,
now transformed into the window of an invisible
showcase housing a part of the collection of
costumes given to the museum by the
Rocamora family*

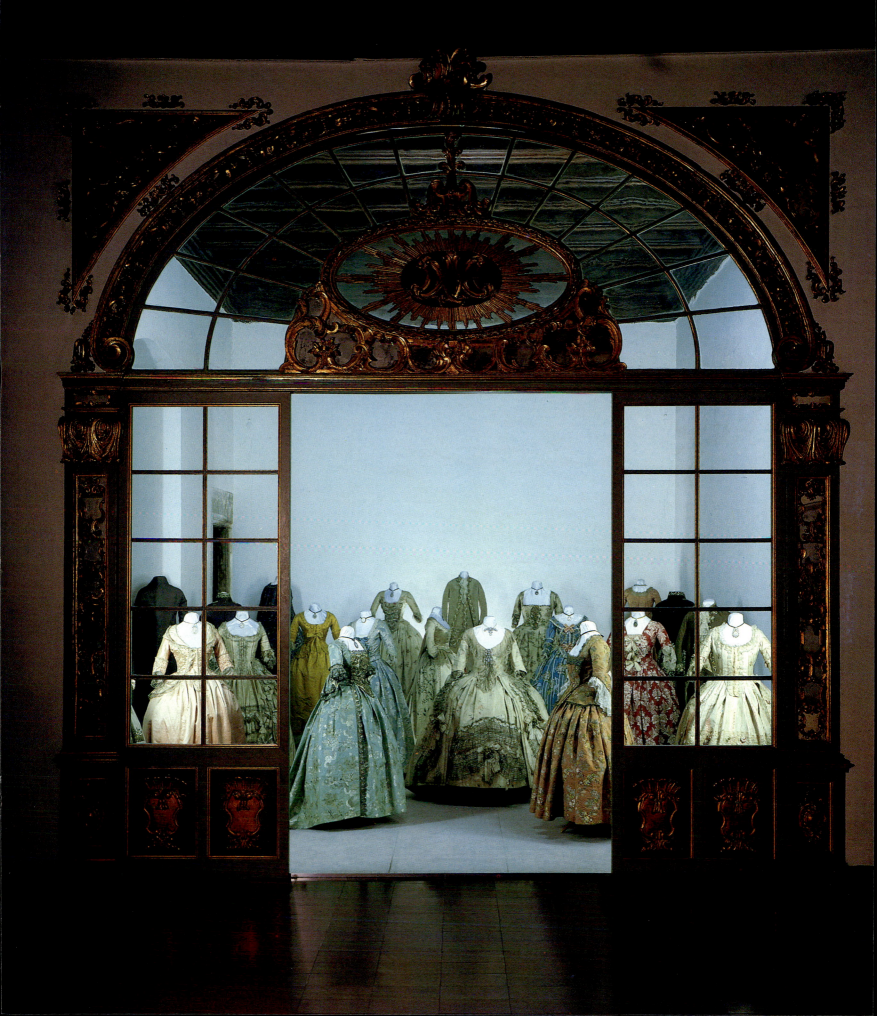

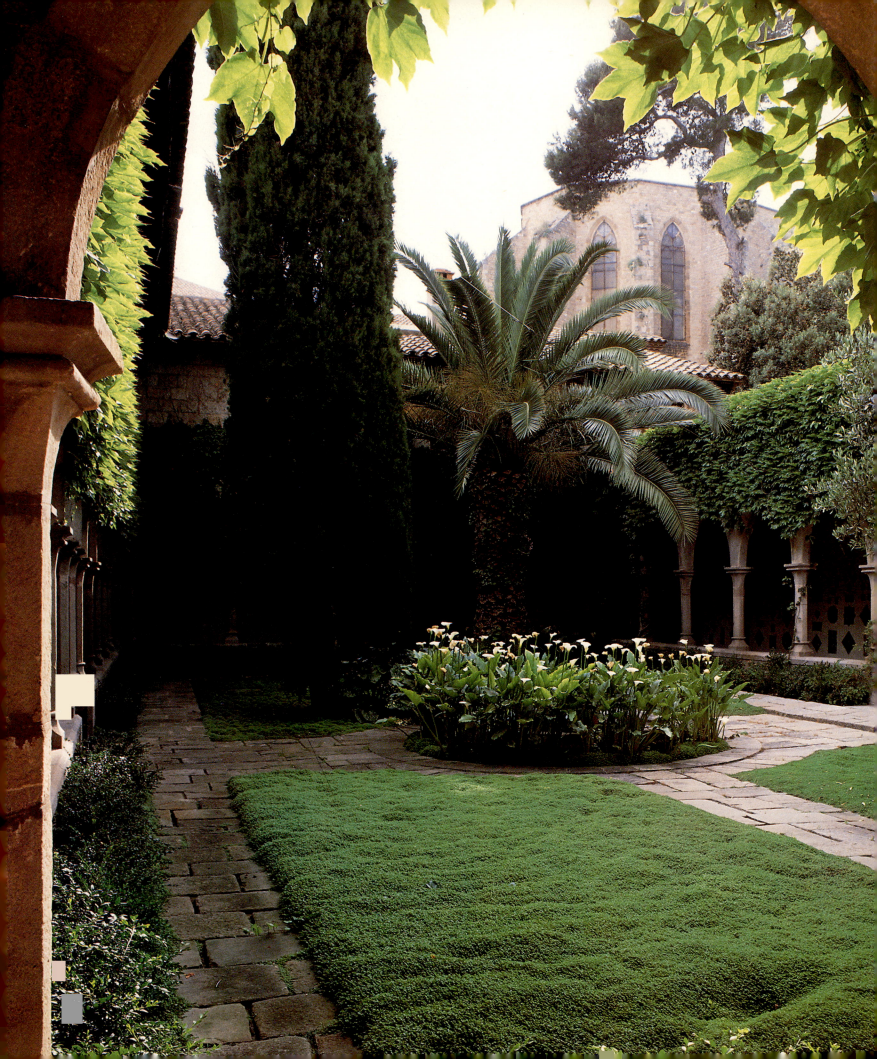

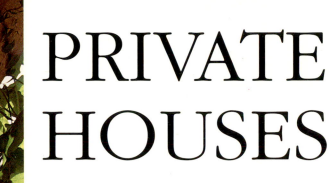

PRIVATE HOUSES

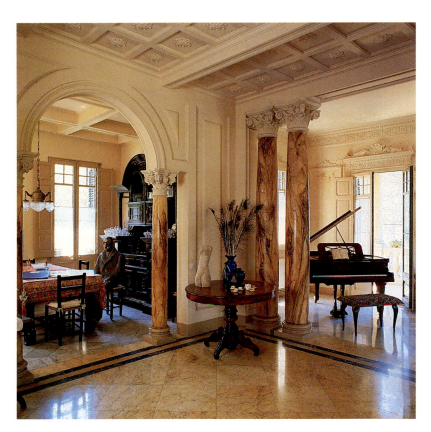

El conventet

*Originally a small Franciscan convent with a
fourteenth-century cloister and chapel, this
extended building now forms a private residence.
The owner, an art collector, has turned his home
into a living museum. The dining room, in daily
use, contains excellent examples of ceramics from
the fourteenth to the nineteenth centuries.*

Casa callejo-amat

*Lost in the woods of Collserola, Casa Callejo-
Amat could tell a few tales of dangerous liaisons
of the past. More modern houses have
encroached since the house was built in 1929
and its walls have suffered damage from the
presence of even older trees. But on a winter
evening today tea and conversation accompanied
by the smell of a freshly baked cake are a
special pleasure.*

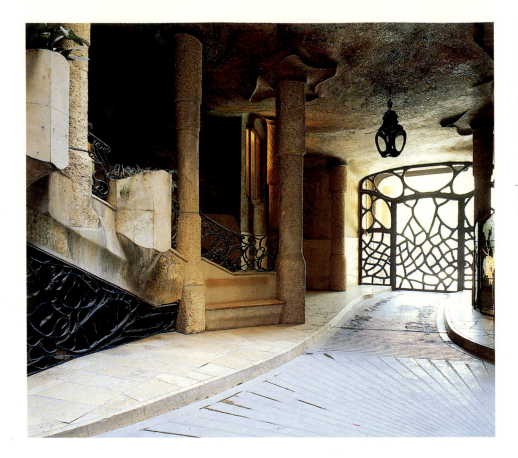

CASA MILÀ

'La Pedrera', one of Gaudí's best works, is important in its own right and for what it represents in the history of architecture and sculpture. Conceived as a whole it is not simply an achievement in private living spaces, but rather an overall piece, though unfinished. When we look at its exterior of stone and iron, its courtyards, roof and chimneys, and at the few flats which have not been altered, we see space and volume forever playing against the light in unforgettable and unrepeatable conjunctions.

CASA SAYRACH

The entrance to any one of the modernista *houses in the* Eixample *is of great interest in itself. Although the 1915 plans were signed by the architect Gabriel Borrell, Casa Sayrach was in fact designed by its present owner Manuel Sayrach, an art lover and great admirer of Gaudí. It was Gaudí's work that inspired the design of this fine entrance hall built in white stone with complicated stucco work, plaster mouldings and ceramic skirting boards.*

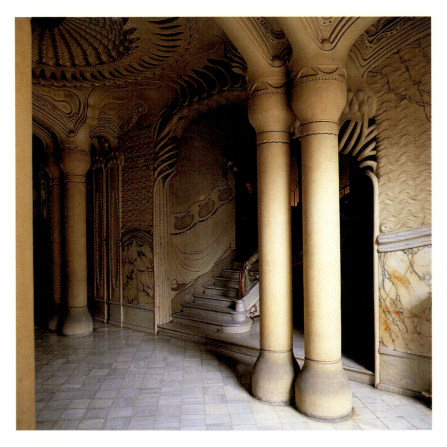

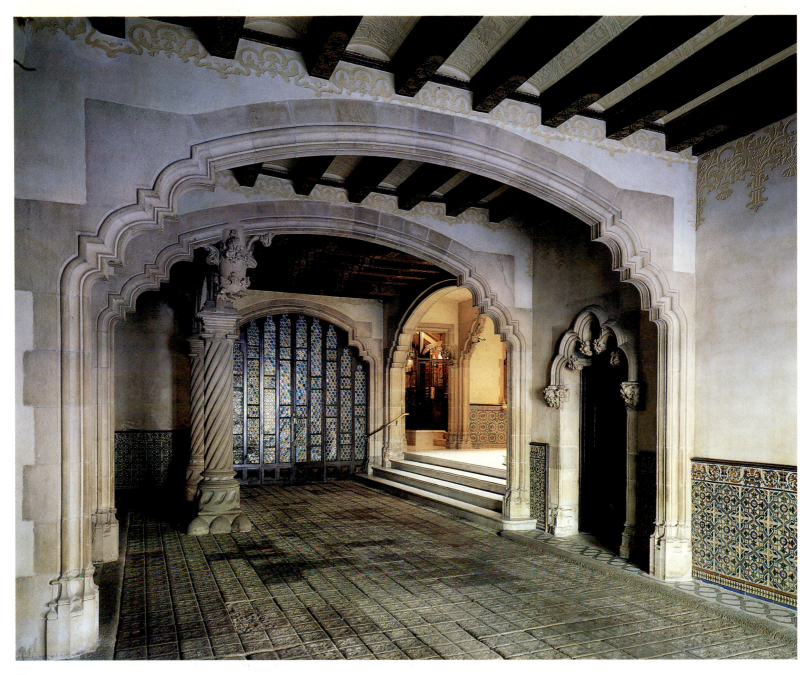

CASA AMATLLER

Architect, archaeologist, politician and historian, Josep Puig i Cadafalch was undoubtedly one of the most versatile figures of his time. In his restoration of the Casa Amatller, between 1898 and 1900, a uniquely creative endeavour, he was able to combine Gothic elements from the Netherlands with Catalan architectural details, not to mention the exceptional iconography found in the sculptural detail. The resulting building brought him recognition as the great interpreter of modernista *neo-Gothic. Seen here, the vestibule, where carriages could enter the ground floor, is especially rich both in the design and in the materials used. Note the finely ornamented ceiling, the noble stone staircase and propitious use of form and colour in the ceramic work.*

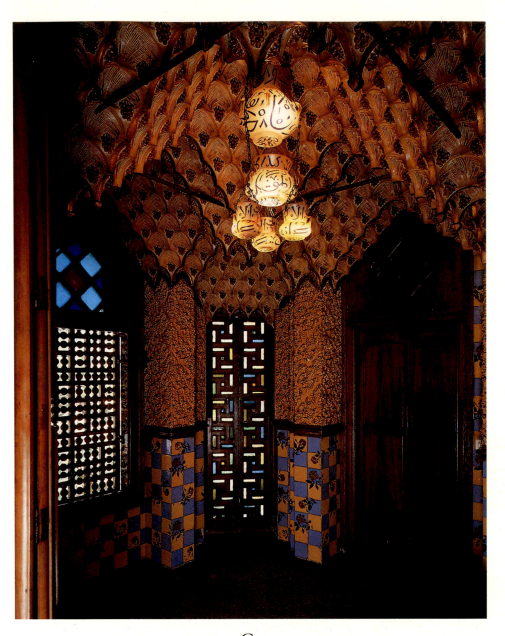

CASA VICENS

This is one of the most surprising houses in the whole of Barcelona. Designed by Gaudí at the end of the last century, it is a daring and personal interpretation of Mudéjar *architecture, the old Christian style which incorporates Islamic ornamental detail. Ceramic elements play with the glass and wooden jalousies to create an oriental mood. In* Mudéjar *style, externally the house is a captivating display of green and white ceramic tiles. In the dining room, this painted ceiling with its* trompe-l'oeil *cupola draws the eye up to a blue sky and flock of birds. Buildings like this demonstrate Gaudí's position not only as the leader of Catalan* Modernisme, *but also of the new style which transformed turn-of-the-century Europe.*

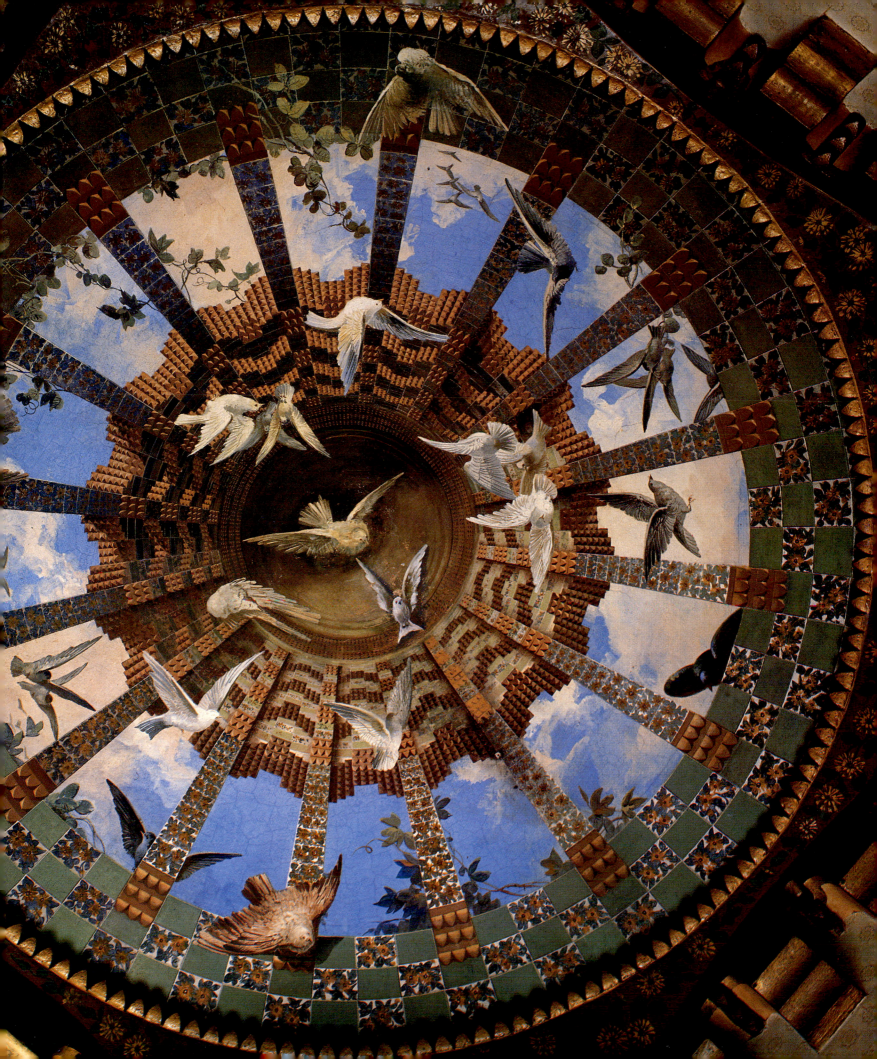

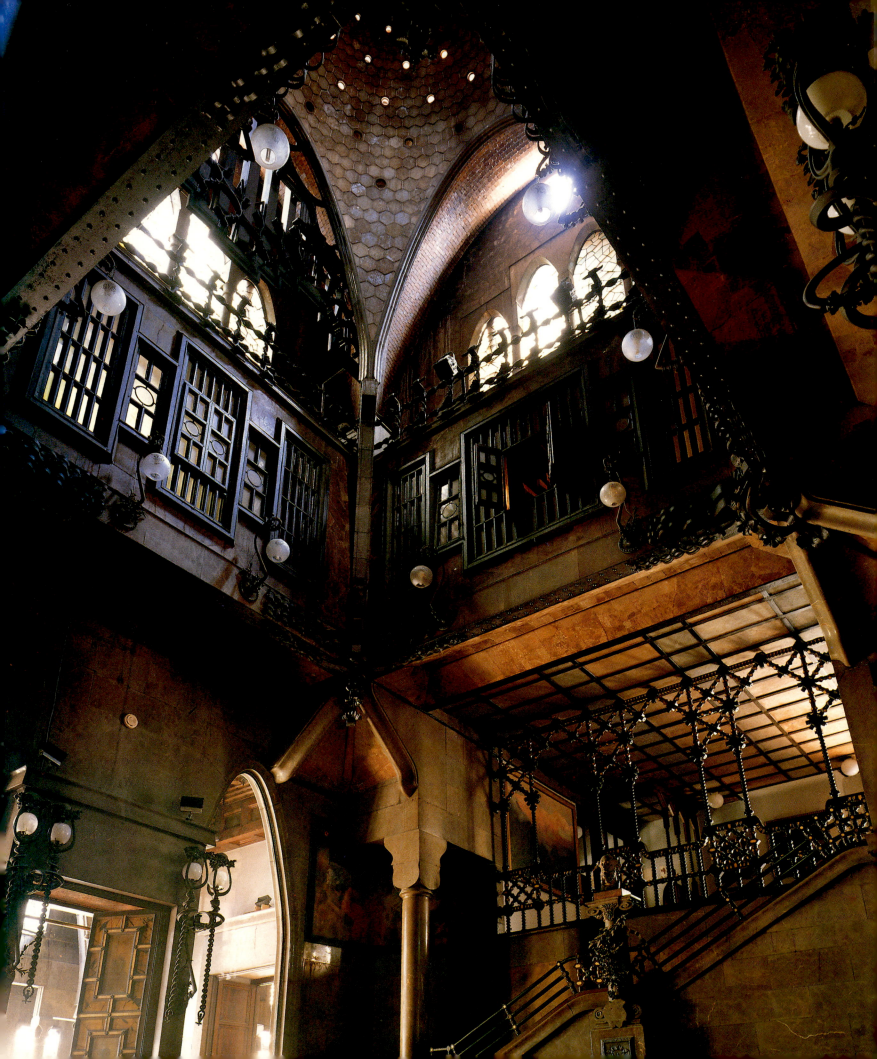

PALAU GÜELL

Just as you begin to lose yourself in the halls of the Palau Güell you start to experience the extraordinary sensation created by a series of horizontal sequences always looking for light at the highest point. Gaudí built this palace for the Counts of Güell between 1885 and 1890 and in this room - both chapel and music room though equally it could be a meeting room or dining room - he used narrow parabolic arches, balustrades, fireplaces and domes, decorated with tiles and stone, to achieve a feeling of continuity. The organic forms are clearly the precedents for the principal elements in Gaudí's later work on the roofs of Casa Batlló and Casa Milà.

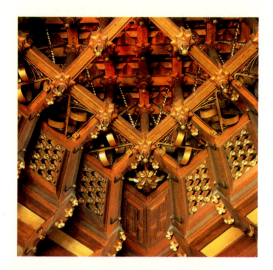

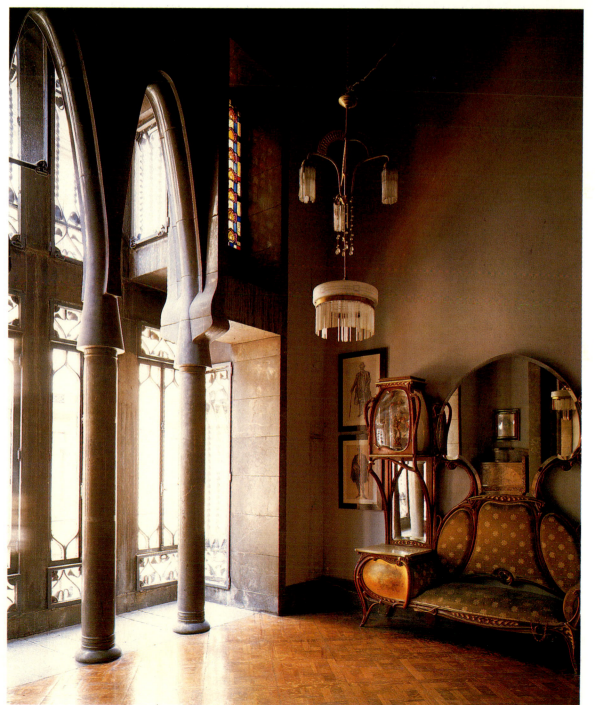

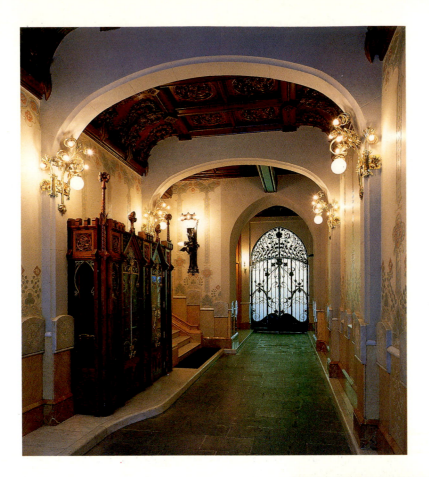

CASA BATLLÓ

Commissioned in the early years of this century by Josep Batlló and recently restored, it would be more accurate to describe this important building by Gaudí as a permanent sculpture rather than a piece of architecture.

The entrance hall to the main area of the first floor is an example of volumetric play of colour, a truly unusual concept, in addition to the skilful use of each material. The shaft of light which appears to be produced between a roof that wants to be a wall and a wall which won't accept the lover's passive horizontal position is a perfect prelude to the love which this passionate construction will be found to contain.

CASA BERENGUER

A family who had been builders since the sixteenth century drew on their tradition and roots to construct this meticulous example of an early twentieth-century house in the Eixample that remains intact today. This building tradition is immediately obvious in the hall where, as in the whole building, the overall construction is more important than the intrinsic artistic value of any one of its component parts, which are at times even bland. What is clear, however, is the high quality of Catalan craftsmanship at the turn of the century in all its facets: in its treatment of glass, wood, metal and stone.

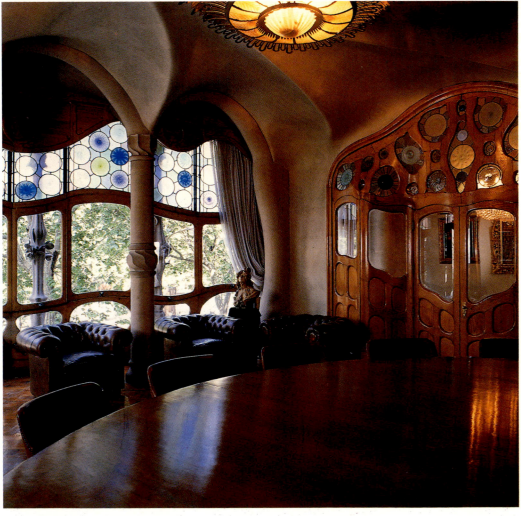

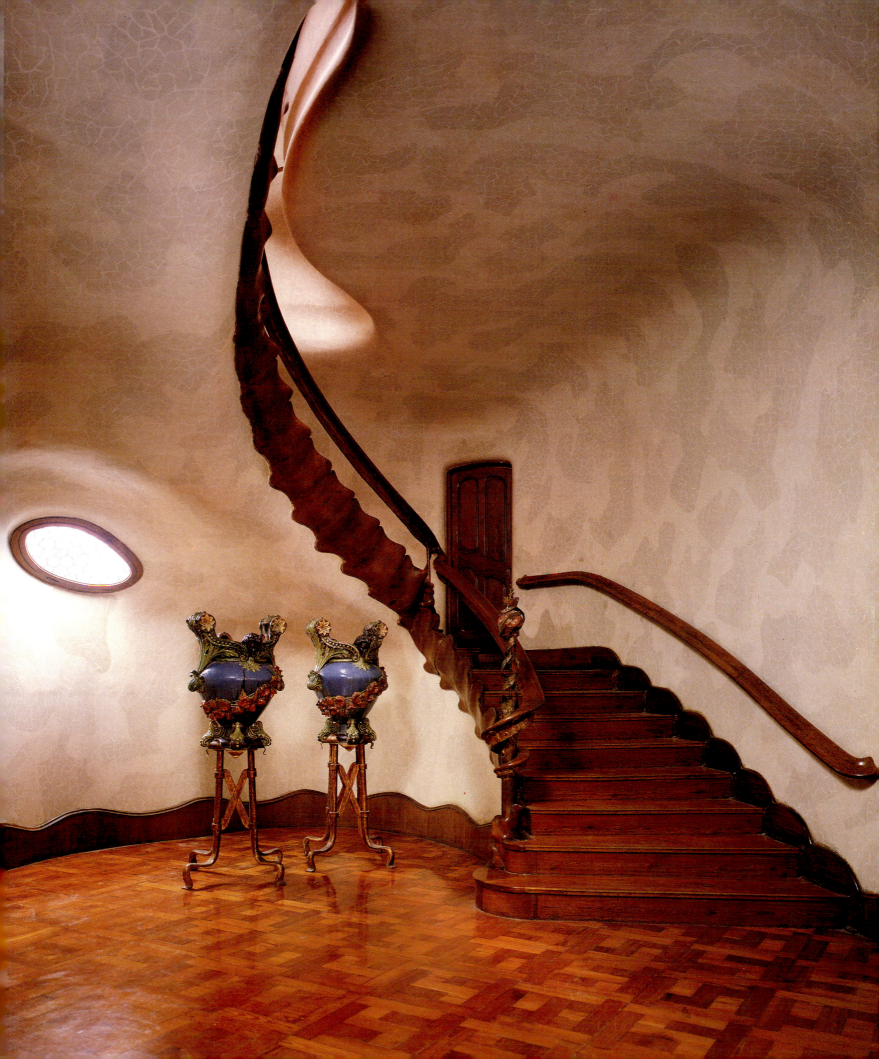

ACKNOWLEDGEMENTS

Writing this book amid the daily routines of an architect's office has been an exciting and, indeed, even a somewhat dizzying experience. Because of this, special thanks are due to some of my colleagues who, with great stoicism and understanding, have accepted the new challenge without letting it get in the way of their regular work.

First I must mention Pilar Breva, my faithful colleague who has been ever attentive to the progress of the book and to its co-ordination. Her common sense and constant good humour made the work altogether happier and more enjoyable for us all.

Next, my secretary, Julia Rosas, whose *savoir-faire* has been unfailing, and who has patiently and efficiently contacted the right person in each public and private organization to arrange appointments and to obtain the necessary permission for us to visit at the exact moment when Peter and I felt the light would be perfect in each of the buildings.

Likewise, thanks to Alex Puig, Ariadna Castelló, Laia Botey, Muriel Botey, Mireia Cumella, Jaume Planas and José Antonio Pérez Breva.

I have intentionally kept Peter Aprahamian's name to the last part of this first acknowledgement. When Peter arrived in Barcelona, commissioned by Phaidon Press to undertake the photography for the book, we explored the streets together, and Peter began to love this town almost as much as I do. And then our visions - mine, his, his, and mine again - became, through the lens, something effortless and enriching for us both, I think. We have worked closely on what has become a sort of dialogue of feelings and images. My thanks go to him, therefore, in the certainty that the acknowledgement is mutual.

Phaidon Press, in the person of Roger Sears, put their faith in me, thus making this third book in the series possible. (*Inside London* and *Inside Paris* are already published.) Together, we have been able to fill a gap in the already extensive bibliography of Barcelona with this useful little book.

Finally, my thanks are due to the extensive group of institutions and friends who have disinterestedly and enthusiastically supported my idea. They have not only opened the doors of their respective properties, but have facilitated access to others. Without their collaboration, these lines would have never been written:

Generalitat de Catalunya, Ajuntament de Barcelona, Arquebisbat de Barcelona, Diputació de Barcelona, Delegació del Govern de Catalunya, Govern Civil de Barcelona; Cambra de Comerç, Indústria i Navegació; Biblioteca del Col.legi d'Arquitectes de Catalunya, Universitat Central de Barcelona; Museums, Official Schools, Schools, Cinemas, Empresa Balañá, Montserrat Abad, Conxa Aguirre, Enric

Alberich, Aurora Altisent, Mr Amat, Lluïsa Amat, Ricardo Ardébol, Margarita Argudo, Mr Aspar, Carme Badia, Endika Barros, Joan Bassegoda, María Teresa Batalla, Mr Batista, Mr Benavent, Enric Bernat, Nina Bernat, Josep María Bilurbina, Montserrat Blanc, Mr Bofarull, Mr Bonilla, Francesc Bosch, Ana Busom, Mr Canela, Mr Carbonell, Mr Carrasco, Montserrat Carreras, Mr Carreras, Jordi Carrió, Teresa Casas, Imma Casas, Josep M. Casaucau, Olga Castall, Ramon Cifuentes, Ramon Clos, Mercedes Comín, Albert Consegal, Joana Crespi, Menchu Cusel, Francesc Cuspinera, Montserrat Dalí, Pilar Duran, Jordi Erce, Teresa Escudé, Mr Espinosa, Josep M. Fargas, Félix Fea, Margarita Ferrer, Roser Forn, Anna Fornesa, Mr Freixenet, Francesc Galmés, Andrea García, Isabel García, Mr García, Airí Garrigosa, Pilar Garrigosa, Mr Ginés Pérez, Pilar Gómez Fuentes, Oriol Granados, Imma Gutiérrez, Antonio Hermesillas, Mrs Herrero, Olga Huguet, Manuel Jorba, Dolors Lamarca, Teresa Lancuentra, Ignacio De Lasaleta, Sergi López, Olga López, Antonio López Roca, Mayo López de María, Francesc Los Huertos, Teresa Lletja, Joan Llobet, Andrés Maeso, Mercè March, Rosa Maria Marsana, Carme Martínez, Mr Martínez, Mr Masllorens, Carles Masa, Montserrat Massó, Mr Méndez, María Angeles Mercader, Eva Mora, Mónica Muñoz, Ramon Negre, Anna Noelle, Maite Ocaña, Pedro Palacios, Carme Palau, Frederic Palau, Mr Pallars, Mr Panyella, María Peña, José Antonio Pérez Torrente, Oriol Pi de Cabanyes, Mr Pitarch, Carles Querol, Josep Ramon Raventós, Miss Redondo, Mr Ribó, Mr Roca, Adela Roche, Mrs Rodríguez, Eduard Roger, Mr Romaní, Josep Rubió, Mar Ruíz, Rosa Sabarich, Mr Sánchez, Gonzalo Sedó, Vda. Segimond, Anna Segués, Salvador Sellent, Francisco Solà, Carme Soldevila, Mr Soler, Jordi Subirà, Enric Tous, Francesc Uribe, Agnès Vendrell, Jaume Vergés, Eli Vidri, Ani Vila, Joan Viña Camprubí, Ernest Xancó, Antoni Zaragoza.

Thanks to my friends Lluis Gelpí, Joan Antoni Solans, Daniel Giralt Miracle, Joan Ainaud de Lasarte and Margarita Tintó who undertook the onerous task of reading and commenting on the manuscript.

Thanks also for the English version to Sheena Baqué, Wendy Farnes, Ann King, John Moran and Teresa Wharmby; for collaboration on the Castillian version to Miquel Dalmau; and for proofreading the Catalan version to Miquel Oller.

BIBLIOGRAPHY

Ainaud, J.F., Ainaud, J., Bassegoda, J., Bonet, J., Cabana, F., Permanyer, L., Rahola, F., Vila i Grau, J., Vila i Delclòs, A.: *La casa Garriga Nogués,* Barcelona, 1990.

Bassegoda, Joan, Casanovas, José, Garrut, José M., Infiesta, J.M., Marco, Joaquín, Socíes, Jaime: *Modernismo en Catalunya,* Barcelona, 1976.

Bohigas, Oriol: *L'architectura del Noucentisme i Novecento,* Barcelona, 1964.

Carandell, Josep M.: *L'Eixample de Barcelona,* Barcelona, 1982.

Catàleg del Patrimoni Arquitectònic Històrico-Artistic de la Ciutat de Barcelona, Barcelona, 1987.

Cirici, Alexandre: *Modernisme i Noucentisme,* Barcelona, 1961.

Cirici, Alexandre, Termes, Josep, Alcolea, Santiago: *La Universidad de Barcelona,* Barcelona, 1971.

Faulí, Josep: *Arquitectura de Barcelona,* Barcelona, 1974.

Fernández, Daniel, Prats, Angels: *Exposició Universal de Barcelona,* 1988.

Flores, Carles: *Gaudí, Jujol y el Modernismo Catalán,* Madrid, 1982.

Fochs, Pere, Jardí, Enric, Lozoya, Antoni, Mascarell, Ferran: *Central Vilanova,* Barcelona, 1987.

Garrut, J.M., Bassegoda, Joan, Porcel, Baltasar, Estapé, Ferran, Wiesental, Mauricio, Valmitjana, Augusto, Castell, Miguel: Barcelona, 1980.

Hernández-Clos, J. Emili, Mora, Gabriel, Pouplana, Xavier: *Arquitectura de Barcelona,* Barcelona, 1972.

Permanyer, Lluís: *Establiments i Negocis que han fet Història,* Barcelona, 1990.

Pomés, Juliet, Fereiche, Ricardo: *Barcelona Design,* Barcelona, 1990.

Pons, Emili, Figueres, Carles, Menade, Maria: *El Comercio de Prestigio en Barcelona,* Barcelona, 1990.

Sobrequés, Jaume, Carandell, Josep M., Caban, Josep, Pérez Puigjané, Manel, Domingo, Magin: *Barcelona Viva,* Barcelona, 1982.

GAZETTEER

Although details are correct at the time of going to press, readers are advised to check opening times etc, before making a visit.
Illustrations in the gazetteer refer to the locations below them.

SHOPS

CASA PALAU
Address: Pl. Reial 8 (08002)
Telephone: 317 07 35 or 317 06 97
Metro: L3 Liceu
Open: 9 am-1.30 pm, 4-7 pm, Mon-Fri.

Exclusive shop and taxidermy workshop; founded in 1889 and moved to the Plaça Reial in 1926.

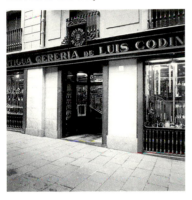

CERERIA SUBIRÀ
Address: Bda. de la Llibreteria 7 (08002)
Telephone: 315 26 06
Metro: L4 Jaume I
Open: 9 am-1.30 pm, 4-7.30 pm, Mon-Fri; 9 am-1.30 pm, Sat.

Family business founded 1761; established as a candlemaker's at the present address in 1909; originally designed in 1847 as a dress shop; preserves interesting elements from that period; restored 1986 by Josep M. Botey.

HERBORISTERIA ENORMES
Address: Ciutat 3 (08002)
Telephone: 302 30 04
Metro: L4 Jaume I
Open: 8 am-1.30 pm, 4-8 pm, Mon-Fri.

Herbalist's shop; one of the oldest shops in the city.

FARMÀCIA MALLOL BALMAÑA
Address: Ferran 7 (08002)
Telephone: 317 22 88
Metro: L4 Jaume I
Open: 9 am-1.30 pm, 4.30-8 pm, Mon-Fri.

Originally known as the Estrella, the first pharmacist set up here in 1842.

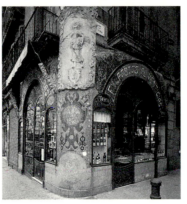

PASTISSERIA ESCRIBA
Address: La Rambla 83 (08002)
Telephone: 301 60 27
Metro: L3 Liceu
Open: 9 am-2 pm, 3.30-8.30 pm, Mon-Fri; 9 am-9 pm, Sat.

The old Figueras patisserie, expanded and restored in 1986 by Christian Escribà; preserves part of the old *modernista* design; mosaic work on the façade is particularly worth noting.

JOIERIA ROCA
Address: Pg. de Gràcia 18 (08007)
Telephone: 318 32 66
Metro: L3/L1 Catalunya
Open: 9.30 am-1.30 pm, 4-8 pm, Mon-Fri.

A good example of rationalism, built by J. Lluís Sert in 1931; the shop is completely different from the average commercial establishment seen today; it retains the tables and chairs of the period.

CASA THOMAS
B.D. Edicions de Disseny
Address: Mallorca 291-293 (08037)
Telephone: 258 69 09
Metro: L5 Verdaguer
Open: 9 am-1.30 pm, 4-7 pm, Mon-Fri.

Original building constructed by Domènech i Montaner between 1895 and 1898; expanded in 1912 by Francesc Guardia; in 1979 the building was awarded the FAD prize for restoration of the ground floor carried out by the PER firm.

CASA BEETHOVEN
Address: La Rambla 97 (08002)
Telephone: 301 48 26
Metro: L3 Liceu or Catalunya
Open: 9 am-1.30 pm, 4-8 pm, Mon-Fri; 9 am-1.30 pm, Sat.

Known as the Casa Beethoven since 1915.

CAMISERIA XANCO
Address: La Rambla 80 (08002)
Telephone: 318 09 89
Metro: L3 Liceu
Open: 10 am-2.30 pm, 4.30-8.30 pm, Mon-Sat.

Shirtmaker's; one of the few old shops left in La Rambla.

VINÇON
Address: Pg. de Gràcia 96 (08008)
Telephone: 215 60 50
Metro: L3 Diagonal
Open: 10 am-2 pm, 4.30-8 pm, Mon-Sat.

Since it opened in 1929 this shop has raised public awareness of design.

CLUBS & INSTITUTIONS

CENTRE CULTURAL DE LA FUNDACIO 'LA CAIXA'
Address: Pg. de Sant Joan 108 (08037)
Telephone: 258 89 07/06
Metro: L4 Verdaguer
Open: 11 am-2 pm, 4-8 pm, Tues-Sat; 10 am-3 pm Sun. and holidays.

Constructed in 1901 by Josep Puíg i Cadafalch, it was declared an Historic-Artistic Monument of National Interest in 1976; one of the finest examples of this architect's *modernista* period; previously known as the Casa Macaya.

CERCLE EQÜESTRE
Address: Balmes 169 (08006)
Telephone: 415 60 00
Metro: L5 Diagonal
Open: 9 am-1 am, every day. Members only.

Known as the Paula Samanillo, built in 1910 by the *modernista* architect Joan Josep Hervàs i Arizmendi; since 1947 the headquarters of the Equestrian Circle; interior, decorated by Joan Esteva, a marvellous collection of numerous rooms, library and music room; note the marble and carved stone staircase.

CERCLE DEL LICEU
Address: La Rambla 63 (08002)
Telephone: 317 41 70
Metro: L3 Liceu
Open: 9 am-1 am. Members only.

Planned when the Liceu was built, this club did not become a reality until 1861, after reconstruction carried out because of fire damage in the Liceu; built in the romantic period within the general movement of the Catalan *Renaixença* (a resurgence in Catalan cultural life); the magnificent stained-glass windows by Antoni Marti and furniture by the Busquets brothers were added in 1862 and the chimney piece in the salon by Francesc Vidal during improvements carried out in 1875. The Ramon Casas picture gallery, the exclusive province of members, is closed to photography.

COL.LEGI D'ADVOCATS
Address: Mallorca 283 (08037)
Telephone: 487 28 14 or 215 67 85
Metro: L5 Verdaguer / L3 Diagonal
Open: during office hours: 9.30 am-2 pm, 4.30-8 pm, Mon-Fri.

The result of an addition to the Palau Casades, this building acquired by the Bar Association in 1922; originally constructed between 1883 and 1885 by Antoni Serra i Pujals, it has a rectangular floor plan with a circular courtyard around which the building is constructed; additions made between 1950 and 1953 by Borrell i Sensat.

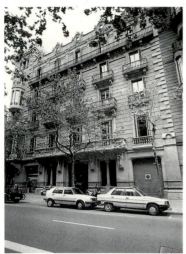

EDITORIAL ENCICLOPEDIA CATALANA
Address: Diputació 250 (080007)
Telephone: 302 71 18
Metro: L4 Passeig de Gràcia
Open: 9 am-8 pm.

Originally Casa Garrigua Nogués designed by Enric Sagnier i Villavechia in 1899; now houses an important publishing house for the promotion of Catalan culture.

REIAL ACADEMIA DE MEDICINA I CIRURGIA
Address: Carme 47 (08001)
Telephone: 317 16 86
Metro: L3 Liceu
Open: 10 am-1 pm, Mon-Fri.

The plans by Ventura Rodríguez date from 1761; building restored in 1929 to make room for the Royal Academy of Medicine; on 2 March 1951 declared an Historic-Artistic Monument of National Interest; note the architectural strength of the cylindrical amphitheatre, lit by a lamp hanging above the operating table and complemented by the Rococo décor.

OMNIUM CULTURAL
Address: Montcada 20 (08003)
Telephone: 319 80 50
Metro: L4 Jaume I
Generally closed to the public.

Original construction dates from the 15th century; in the 17th century it was completely renovated; a fine example of Barcelonian Baroque known as the Palau Dalmases, it hasbeen the successive headquarters of the Academy of the Untrusting,

the Academy of Letters and, since 1962, the Omnium Cultural.

CENTRE EXCURSIONISTA DE CATALUNYA
Address: Paradís 10 (08002)
Telephone: 315 23 11
Metro: L4 Jaume I
Open: 6 pm-9 pm, Mon-Fri.

Founded in 1876, this club for intrepid travellers was moved almost immediately to this building whose original construction dates from the 13th and 14th centuries; restored in 1905; represents one of the best examples of medieval secular architecture in private use in Barcelona; interior courtyard boasts four columns from the Roman temple of Augustus.

THEATRES, CINEMAS & MUSIC HALLS

PALAU DE LA MUSICA CATALANA
Address: Sant Francesc de Pàola 2 (08003)
Telephone: 268 10 00 or 301 11 04
Metro: L4 Urquinaona
Open: 3 and 4 pm, Tues and Fri; 10, 11 pm and 12 noon, Sat.
Visits, with guide, must be prearranged; telephone for details.

Fostered by the Orfeó Català (an institution formed in 1891) this was to be 'la nostra casa', the temple of Catalan art and the palace of the Catalan Renaixença; built between 1905 and 1908 by Domenech i Montaner, the concert hall, built of iron with large glass panes, is the building's focal point; refurbished in 1989 by Oscar Tusquets for which it won the FAD restoration award.

GRAN TEATRE DEL LICEU
Address: La Rambla 63 (08002)
Telephone: 318 91 22
Metro: L3 Liceu
Open: 11.30 am and 12.15 pm, Mon-Fri. Visits prearranged; telephone for details.

Original building designed by Miquel Garriga after the tradition of the French opera houses; destroyed by fire on 9 April 1861; rebuilt by Josep Oriol Mestres and reopened on 20 April 1862; (see also CERCLE DEL LICEU).

TEATRE TIVOLI
Address: Casp 10 (08010)
Telephone: 215 95 70 or 318 60 98
Metro: L3/L1 Catalunya
Open: every day from 4.30 pm.

Cinema built between 1917 and 1919 by Miquel Madorell i Rius; note the large glassed areas framed by the arrangement of enormous columns and the majestic staircase to the upper floors.

LA PALOMA
Address: Tigre 27 (08001)
Telephone: 301 68 97 or 317 79 94
Metro: L1 Universitat
Open: from 9 pm, Sat and Sun only.

The old Comas establishment; decorated by Salvador Alarma i Moragas 1919; Manuel Mestre redecorated the hall with relief work, gold paint, mouldings and the chandelier which is still in place.

EL MOLINO
Address: Vila i Vilà 99 (08004)
Telephone: 329 88 54 or 441 63 83
Metro: L3 Paral.lel
Open: every day from 6 pm except Mon.

Built by the *modernista* architect Raspall in 1910, the stage and orchestra pit were known as 'The Aviary'.

TEATRE ARNAU
Address: Av. Paral.lel 60 (08001)
Telephone: 442 28 04
Metro: L3 Paral.lel
Open: every day after 9 pm.

Once a cinema, has been a music hall since the 1970s.

BANKS OFFICES & STATIONS

BANCA CATALANA
Address: La Rambla 102 (08002)
Telephone: 301 75 24
Metro: L3 Liceu
Banking Hall open: 8.30 am-2 pm, Mon-Fri

Constructed in 1874 as the head offices of the Banca Mas Sardà, a large part of the original construction has been retained in a restoration carried out with the greatest respect for the exquisite interior.

CONVENTION BUREAU
Address: Pg. de Gràcia 35 (08007)
Telephone: 215 44 77
Metro: L3 Passeig de Gràcia
Open: during office hours: 8 am-3 pm, Mon-Fri.

Originally the Casa Lleó Morera; one of the best examples of Catalan *Modernisme* the result of remodelling done by Domènech i Montaner between 1902 and 1906 of one of the first houses built in this street in 1864; current decoration of the meeting room is the work of Barcelona Design, by the interior designer Mireia Riera; houses the city's tourist board.

HERON BUILDING
Address: Av. Diagonal 605 (08028)
Telephone: 239 07 01 or 322 10 00
Metro: L3 Maria Cristina
Open: during office hours.

High-tech building constructed 1987-88 by Josep Maria Fargas and Enric Tous; unique are elements such as the staircase and skylight over the courtyard.

LLOTJA
Address: Pg. d'Isabel II, 4 (08003)
Telephone: 319 24 12
Metro: L4 Barceloneta
Open: 10-12 am, Mon-Fri; guided visits. Telephone for details.

The old Barcelona Exchange designed in 1339 by the Consell dels Vint; the Trading Room created in 1383 by Pere Arbei; Joan Soler drew up the plans in 1764 for the expansion project and directed the construction between 1772 and 1794; a provisional bunker during the reign of Felip V, it was declared an Historic-Artistic Monument 1931.

ESTACIO DE FRANÇA
Address: Pl. d'Ocata 5 (08003)
Telephone: 319 98 85
Metro: L4 Barceloneta
Admission: by written request.

In 1848 the first Spanish railway line, between Barcelona and Mataró, left from a tiny station very near the current one; in 1923 construction begun on a central railway station, one of the largest in Europe; this iron building the work of the engineer Aneru Montaner; of interest: the impressive hall, the façade, the curved vaulted ceilings and twelve tracks; technically one of the most advanced stations; station is built on a curve.

AIGÜES DE BARCELONA
Address: Pg. de Sant Joan 39 (08009)
Telephone: 265 80 11
Metro: L5 Verdaguer
Open: during office hours: 8.30 am-2.30 pm, Mon-Fri.

Built at the turn of the century and taken over by the municipal water company; all the various restorations have left the original structure intact; the magnificent iron glasshouse was constructed in 1868 and remodelled by Antoni Muntanyà.

SCHOOLS & COLLEGES

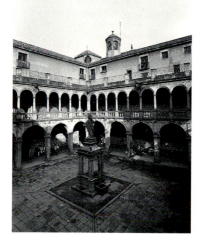

UNIVERSITAT CENTRAL DE BARCELONA
Address: G.V. de les Corts Catalanes 585 (08007)
Telephone: 318 42 66
Metro: L1 Universitat
Visits on written request.

The most outstanding building by Elies Rogent, whose ideas derived from Viollet-le-Duc, was inspired by the architecture of the 15th century, that is, late Gothic and proto-Renaissance; oriental influence can be seen in the Nazarene decoration of the Paranimf auditorium.

COL.LEGI DE LES TERESIANES
Address: Ganduxer 105 (08022)
Telephone: 212 33 54
Metro: L-Sarrià, La Bonanova
Admission: by prior arrangement.

Built by Antoni Gaudí between 1889 and 1894; in 1969 declared an Historic-Artistic Monument; now

one of the most renowned girls' schools in the city.

ESCOLA DELS JESUITES DE SARRIÀ
Address: Carrasco i Formiguera 32 (08017)
Telephone: 203 90 16
Metro: L-Sarrià, Sarrià
Admission: by prior arrangement.

Neo-Gothic Tudor structure built between 1893 and 1896 by Joan Martorell; the Company of Jesus commissioned construction in 1893.

GRUP ESCOLAR PERE VILA
Address: Pg. de Lluís Companys 18 (08003)
Telephone: 309 94 17
Metro: L1 Arc de Triomf
Admission: by prior arrangement. Telephone for details.

State school designed by Josep Goday i Casals in *noucentista* style during the 1920s; school building and library funded by businessman and philanthropist Pere Vila i Codina.

ESCOLA DEL TREBALL
Address: Comte d'Urgell 187 (08036)
Telephone: 430 16 04
Metro: L5 Hospital Clínic
Open: every day

School of Engineering built between 1927 and 1931 by Joan Rubió i Vallbé, forming part of large complex made up of clock building, technical engineering school and fine crafts school; in 1961 Manuel Baldrich added the new pavilion; entrance to the school is covered with a parabolic form of diaphragmatic arches and a ceiling allowing daylight to penetrate; surface and coffer work are *noucentista;* Casajoana i Salvi is currently restoring the building.

HOTELS & HOSTELS

HOTEL RITZ
Address: Roger de Llúria 28 (08010)
Telephone: 318 52 00
Metro: L1 Urquinaona

Designed by Francesc Folguera in 1917, constructed under the direction of Eduard Ferrés (1917-19), the Hotel Ritz of Barcelona introduces its guests to the French

style and a décor which reflects the atmosphere of the palaces of the old nobility.

HOTEL COMTES DE BARCELONA
Address: Pg. de Gràcia 75 (08008)
Telephone: 487 37 37
Metro: L3 Passeig de Gràcia

The old Casa Enric Batlló by the architect Josep Vilaseca was completed in 1896; pre-*modernista* in style, the façade, entrance, foyer and interior courtyard are considered to be part of the architectural and artistic heritage; building included in the Quadrat d'Or (Golden Square); refurbishing and remodelling begun to convert it into the Hotel Comtes de Barcelona in 1985, work that was carried out by the architect Josep Joanpera; received the Catalan tourism diploma (1987); Rehabitec awarded it a diploma for refurbishment and change of use in 1988.

HOTEL ORIENTE
Address: La Rambla 45-47 (08002)
Telephone: 302 25 58
Metro: L3 Liceu

Once the old Escola Sant Bonaventura, founded by the Franciscans in 1652, the cloisters are currently the hotel ballroom; as early as 1842 it was well known as the Fonda del Oriente.

HOTEL ESPAÑA
Address: Sant Pau 9-11 (08001)
Telephone: 318 17 58
Metro: L3 Liceu

Prize-winning building in 1904, this hotel is a masterpiece among Catalan *modernista* interiors; constructed in 1900 as the Fonda España by Lluís Domènech i Montaner who was responsible for the decoration; the most important and valuable piece is the gigantic fireplace by Eusebi Arnau.

ALBERG MARE DE DÉU DEL COLL
Address: Pg. Mare de Déu del Coll 41 (08023)
Telephone: 210 51 51 or 213 86 33
Metro: L3 Vallcarca

Constructed in 1907 as the summer home of the Marsans family, this *modernista* building was later a convent and then an orphanage for twenty years; during the Civil War

used as a social services centre and converted in 1983 into a youth hostel; note the neo-Arabian entrance.

BARS & RESTAURANTS

BRASSERIE FLO
Address: Jonqueres 10 (08003)
Telephone: 317 80 37
Metro: L1/L4 Urquinaona
Open: 1.30-4 pm, 8.30 pm-midnight, daily.

Located in a 19th-century building which was an old textile warehouse, the design of this restaurant inspired by turn-of-the-century French brasseries the interior space, which combines *modernista* motifs with secessionist elements, was created in 1982 by Antoni de Moragas i Spa.

ELS QUATRE GATS
Address: Montsió 3 (08002)
Telephone: 302 41 40
Metro: L1/L3 Catalunya
Open: 1 pm-4 pm, 9 pm-midnight, Mon-Sat; 6 pm-midnight, Sun.

Puig i Cadalfach's first important work, built 1885-86; declared an Historic-Artistic Monument in 1976; decoration conceptually neo-Gothic with a free interpretation of typical Catalan architecture and elements of *Modernisme.*

EL FRARE BLANC (EL ASADOR DE ARANDA)
Address: Av. del Tibidabo 31 (08022)
Telephone: 417 01 15
Metro: L-Tibidabo, Tibidabo
Open: 1-4 pm, 9 pm-midnight, Mon-Sat; 1-4 pm, Sun.

Built by Joan Rubió i Bellvé between 1903 and 1913 and given an award by the city council in 1914, it was rehabilitated and converted into a restaurant in 1987-88, by Moragas, Bonet i Milà; known as the El Frare Blanc, the house formerly belonged to a Dominican convent; the last and most representative work of Rubió i Bellvé's *modernista* period.

BELTXENEA
Address: Mallorca 275 (08008)
Telephone: 215 30 24
Metro: L3 Passeig de Gràcia
Open: 1.30-4 pm, 9-11.15 pm, Mon-Fri; 9-11.15 pm, Sat.

Distinguished private house converted into a restaurant.

AZULETE
Address: Via Augusta 281 (08017)
Telephone: 203 59 43
Metro: L-Sarrià, Tres Torres
Open: 2-4 pm, 9 pm-midnight, Mon-Fri; 9 pm-midnight, Sat.

Modernista house with a dining area under a large glass structure in the garden; Oscar Tusquets, Ignacio Paricio and Pepe Cortés received the FAD interior decoration award in 1983 for this project.

LOS CARACOLES
Address: Escudellers 14 (08002)
Telephone: 302 31 85 or 301 20 41
Metro: L3 Liceu
Open: 1.30 pm-midnight daily.

In its 160-year history, Los Caracoles (The Snails) started as a shop and wine cellar; now an extremely popular restaurant which has been frequented by many celebrities; décor still has an air of the simple establishment it once was.

NETWORK
Address: Av. Diagonal 616 (08021)
Telephone: 201 72 38
Metro: L5 Hospital Clínic
Open: 1-4pm, 8.30 pm-1 am, Mon Thurs. and Sun; 1-4 pm, 8.30 pm-2 am, Fri-Sat.

Restaurant-music bar with an exciting atmosphere extremely well designed by Eduard Samsó and Alfred Arribas in the late 1980s.

NICK HAVANNA
Address: Rosselló 208 (08008)
Telephone: 215 65 91
Metro: L3 Diagonal
Open: 8 am-3 pm, Mon-Thurs; 8 am-4 pm, Fri-Sat; 7 am-3 pm, Sun.

One of the genuine 'design' bars which has become a must for tourists; designed by Eduard Samsó in 1986.

ZSA-ZSA
Address: Rosselló 156 (08036)
Telephone: 453 85 66
Metro: L5 Hospital Clínic
Open: 7 pm-3 am, Mon-Fri; 7 pm-4 am, Sat-Sun.

Cocktail bar designed in 1989 by Dani Freixes and Vicente Miranda; the methacrylate-lined wall and light play are worth mentioning.

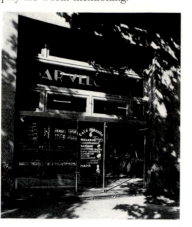

VELODROM
Address: Muntaner 221 (08036)
Telephone: 430 60 22
Metro: L3 Diagonal
Open: 6 pm-2 am, Mon-Sat.

Café-bar from the 1940s in the style of post-war social club bars.

CAFE DEL CENTRE
Address: Girona 69 (08009)
Telephone: 302 10 12
Metro: L4 Girona
Open: 8 am - midnight, Mon-Sat.

During the Republic a casino where a great deal of heavy gambling took place; later turned into a wine cellar and café.

LIBRARIES & ARCHIVES

BIBLIOTECA DE CATALUNYA
Address: Carme 47 (08001)
Telephone: 317 07 78
Metro: L3 Liceu
Open: 9 am-8 pm, Mon-Fri; 9 am-2 pm, Sat.

The old Hospital de la Santa Creu, founded in 1401, built according to a medieval model with two-storey bays around a rectangular cloister; in 1968 Adolf Florensa restored it for use as the Library of Catalonia; currently houses in addition various cultural institutions; declared an Historical-Artistic Monument of National Interest in 1931.

ARXIU FOTOGRÀFIC MAS
Address: Freneria 5 (08002)
Telephone: 315 27 06
Metro: L4 Jaume I
Open: 9 am-2.30 pm, Mon-Fri.

Photographic archive of Catalonia, in particular Barcelona. Complete photographic record of the province's past.

CASA DE L'ARDIACA
Address: Santa Llucia 1 (08002)
Telephone: 318 11 95
Metro: L4 Jaume I
Open 9 am-8.30 pm, Mon-Fri; 9 am-1 pm, Sat. Visits by arrangement.

Catalan Gothic building dating from the 12th and 13th centuries; after various alterations and extensions declared an Historic-Artistic Monument in 1924; note the Golden Pine Cones Room, the spiral staircase leading to the upper floors and the arched gallery.

BIBLIOTECA DE L'ATENEU
Address: Canuda 6 (08002)
Telephone: 318 86 34 or 317 49 04
Metro: L3 Catalunya
Open: 9 am-1.30 pm, Mon-Fri; 9 am-11 pm, Sat. Sun.

Palace designed in 1796 by Josep Francesc Ferrer de Llupià; refurbished between 1904 and 1906 by Josep Font i Josep Maria Jujol and in 1969 by Joan Bassegoda and Adolf Florensa; still remaining of the old palace are the façade, the entrance, the romantic garden and the pictorial decoration by Francesc Pla, 'El Vigatà'; now houses the Barcelona Atheneum, a cultural society formed in 1872.

BIBLIOTECA DE LA UNIVERSITAT
Address: G.V. de les Corts Catalanes 585 (08007)
Telephone: 318 42 66
Metro: L1 Universitat
Open: 8 am-9.15 pm, Mon-Fri; 9 am-1 pm, Sat.

Built in 1865 to a design by Elies Rogent; in 1923 the skylight was altered; Josep González and Francesc Perales, of GATCPAC, were responsible for the plans of the library.

BIBLIOTECA DEL COL.LEGI D'ADVOCATS
Address: Mallorca 283 (08037)
Telephone: 487 28 14 or 215 67 85
Metro: L5 Verdaguer L3 Diagonal
Open: 9 am-2 pm, 4-9 pm, Mon-Fri.

Library of the Bar Association found within the Palau Cassades.

GOVERNMENT & CIVIC BUILDINGS

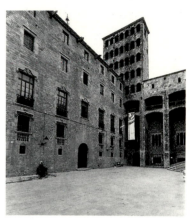

PALAU DE LA GENERALITAT DE CATALUNYA
Address: Pl. de Sant Jaume, s/n (08002)
Telephone: 402 46 00 or 404 46 00
Metro: L4 Jaume I
Open: Sat., Sun. by written request.

Original building dates from the end of the 14th century; Marc Safont constructed the façade on to Bisbe in 1418, the courtyard and the stairway in 1429, and the Sant Jordi chapel in 1434; over the centuries extended and enriched: the Pati dels Tarongers (Orange Grove Courtyard) and the Cambra Daurada (Golden Room) built at the beginning of the 16th century; in 1617 Pere Blay constructed the façade to Plaça Sant Jaume; declared an Historic-Artistic Monument of National Interest in 1931; built as the Catalan government headquarters, which it still is.

HIDROLECTRICA DE CATALUNYA

Address: Av. Vilanova 12-14 (08018)
Telephone: 309 50 50
Metro: L1 Arc de Triomf
Open: during office hours,
8.30 am-1.30 pm, Mon.-Fri.

Original thermal centre, work of Pere Falqués i Urpi in 1897, extended in 1910 by Telm Fernández, it now houses the central administration of Hidroelèctrica de Catalunya. Restored 1977-80 by engineers J.M. Sanz and A. Torra, architect A. Lozoya and the interior designer P. Fochs, resulting in the award of the Premi Amics de la Ciutat.

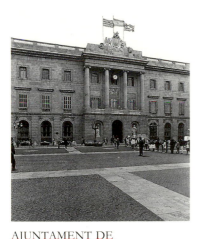

AJUNTAMENT DE BARCELONA

Address: Pl. de Sant Jaume 1 (08002)
Telephone: 302 42 00 or 302 61 45
Metro: L4 Jaume I
Open: prearranged guided visits, Mon-Fri, mornings.

Although this building's origins are hazy, the Saló de Cent by Pere Llobet, constructed in 1372, is one of the most prized examples of secular Catalan Gothic. The Gothic façade on Carrer de la Ciutat dates from 1399 to 1402; successive extensions and restorations took place until mid 19th century when Josep Mas i Vila built the main façade on to Plaça Sant Jaume; further restoration carried out by Lluís Domènech i Montaner for the 1888 Universal Exhibition, and by Antoni de Falguera, Joaquim Vilaseca and Adolf Florensa on the occasion of the 1929 International Exhibition.

PALAU REIAL MAJOR

Address: Pl. del Rei, s/n (08002)
Metro: L4 Jaume I

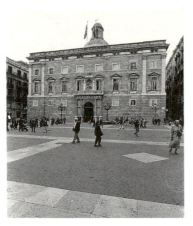

Neo-classical building designed by Josep and Pau Mas i Dordal (1774-90); loggia constructed in 1856 by Rovira i Trias; restored in 1983-84 by F. Mitjans i Miró to house the Department of Culture of the Generalitat.

PALAU DE PEDRALBES

Address: Av. Diagonal 686 (08034)
Telephone: 280 19 64
Metro: L3 Palau Reial
Closed to the public.

Casa Güell, refurbished and expanded, was converted to form the residence of the Spanish royal family between 1919 and 1929 by Eusebi Bona and Puig i Francesc de P. Nebot; in 1931 declared an Historic-Artistic Monument of National Interest; in 1960 opened to the public; currently houses the Ceramics Museum on the first floor; institutional receptions held in its other rooms; stables refurbished in 1985 by the architect Antoni Carrió.

PALAUET ALBENIZ

Address: Pg. Santa Madrona, s/n (08004)
Telephone: 325 90 00
Metro: L1 Plaça Espanya
Admission must be prearranged in writing.

Built in 1928 by Joan Moya; restoration carried out by Joaquín Ros de Ramis, Ignacio María de la Serra Godoy and Antonio Lozoya; dome above the entrance hall painted by Dalí.

GOVERN CIVIL

Address: Av. Marquès de l'Argentera 2 (08003)
Telephone: 319 25 00
Metro: L4 Barceloneta
Open: by appointment.

Constructed to replace the old

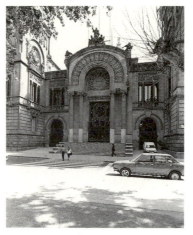

Customs House between 1790 and 1792 by Count Roncali; built during the Neo-classical period, it is a throwback to the Vitruvian classicist school; restored in 1986 by Lluís Gelpí i Vintró.

PALAU DE JUSTICIA

Address: Pg. de Lluís Companys 14 (08018)
Telephone: 309 91 23
Metro: L1 Arc de Triomf
Admission: by previous written request.

Constructed between 1887 and 1908 by Josep Domènech i Estepà and Enric Sagnier i Villavechia; chronologically one of the first defining works of architectural *Modernisme,* but with thematic suggestions of the French and Anglo-Saxon styles; note the entrance steps and the grand staircase leading to the main floor.

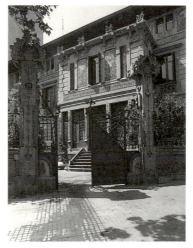

DELEGACIO DEL GOVERN A CATALUNYA

Address: Mallorca, 278 08037
Telephone: 487 22 33
Metro: L5 Verdaguer
Open: by appointment.

The old Palau Montaner designed by Josep Domènech i Estapà in 1889;

completed by Domènech i Montaner in 1891-93; an early example of the *modernista* and *pre-modernista* dialectic; in the interior, note the spatial and decorative richness of the entrance hall and staircase and overhanging passageway lit by a large glass skylight.

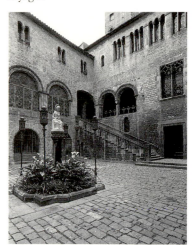

PALAU EPISCOPAL

Address: Bisbe 5 (08002)
Telephone: 318 30 31 or 318 16 79
Metro: L4 Jaume I
Open: by appointment.

The first episcopal palace dates from the 12th century; later moved to another building attached to the towers of the Roman wall; in the new palace, note the large room decorated at the end of the 17th century by the late Baroque painter Francesc Pla, 'El Vigatà'.

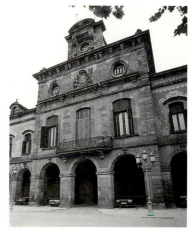

PARLAMENT DE CATALUNYA

Address: Parc de la Ciutadella (08003)
Telephone: 300 62 63
Metro: L4 Ciutadella
Open: by appointment.

Built between 1716 and 1727 as the arsenal of the Ciutadella; in 1962 declared an Historic-Artistic Monument of National Interest; in

1980 finally refurbished as the headquarters of the Parlament of Catalonia; building has two two-storey vaulted galleries laid out in the form of a cross in the classical French style.

DIPOSIT DE LES AIGÜES
Address: Wellington 48 (08005)
Metro: L4 Ciutadella
Open: by appointment with written request

Unique brick building constructed for the Ciutadella Park water supply between 1874 and 1877 by the architect Josep Fontserè i Mestres with Antoni Gaudí as assistant when still a student; refurbished and expanded in 1988 by Lluís Clotet i Ballús and Ignacio Paricio i Ansuastegui.

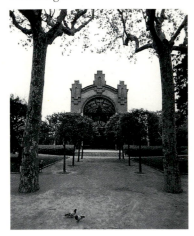

UMBRACLE
Address: Parc de la Ciutadella (08003)
Telephone: 424 38 09
Metro: L1 Arc de Triomf
Open: 9 am-2 pm, Mon-Fri.

In 1883-84, Josep Fontserè i Mestres built this glasshouse with a lobed section and cast-iron columns, curved metal cables and wooden boards.

HOSPITALS & RESIDENCES

HOSPITAL DE LA SANTA CREU I SANT PAU
Address: Sant Antoni Maria Claret 167 (08025)
Telephone: 347 31 33
Metro: L5 Hospital de Sant Pau
Open: every day

First pavilions built 1902-11 by Lluís Domènech i Montaner; work continued by his son, Pere Domènech i Roura; an important

hospital, both architecturally and for its work; declared an Historic-Artistic Monument in 1978; of special interest: the entrance hall of the administration pavilion, the meeting room, the library and the secretary's office.

CLINICA BARRAQUER
Address: Muntaner 314 (08021)
Telephone: 209 53 11
Metro: L-Sarrià, Muntaner
Open: by appointment

This building (1934-40) designed by Joaquim Lloret i Homs, incorporates formal elements characteristic of European Expressionism as well as the Academicist tradition; used as a consulting room, ophthalmological clinic and Dr. Barraquer's private house.

RESIDENCIA FRANCESC LAYRET
Address: G.V. de les Corts Catalanes 475-477 (08015)
Metro: L1 Urgell
Not open to visitors

Constructed 1910-13 by Antoni de Falguera i Sivilla and Falqués i Urpi and built round a large courtyard which serves as an entrance hall; note the impressive façade; now a retirement home.

CONSELLERIA DE SANITAT DE LA GENERALITAT DE CATALUNYA
Address: Trav. de les Corts 131-159 (08028)
Telephone: 339 11 11
Metro: L3 Les Corts
Closed to visitors.

Known as the Provincial House of Maternity, and constructed between 1883 and 1902, the work of Camil Oliveras; extended in 1924 by Josep Goday, the whole building was restored in 1983 by the architects Josep M. Botey, Andreu Bosch and Lluís Cuspinera to house the Health Department; winner of the FAD award in 1983 for restoration.

MUSEUMS

FUNDACIO JOAN MIRÓ
Address: Parc de Montjuïc, s/n (08004)
Telephone: 329 19 08
Metro: L3 Espanya, then Bus 61
Open: 11 am-7 pm daily.

Designed in 1972-74 by Josep Lluís Sert and Associates and subsequently extended in 1988 by Jaume Freixas; houses the art collection donated by Joan Miró; Sert, a friend of the artist, had built Miró's studio in Mallorca and attempted here to conciliate the modern movement with the features of popular Mediterranean architecture; note the powerful filtered light, one of the building's finest qualities.

MUSEU D'ART DE CATALUNYA
Address: Mirador del Palau 6 (08004)
Telephone: 423 71 99 or 325 56 35
Metro: L1 Espanya
Presently undergoing restoration.

Designed by Enric Catà and Pedro Cendoya in 1925; in 1962 declared an Historic-Artistic Monument; at present being remodelled by Gea Aulenti; a stylistic synthesis of several models of Spanish architecture; note the entrance hall, the grand double staircase, the Francesc Galí dome and the oval room, one of the largest in Europe.

MUSEU D'HISTORIA DE LA CIUTAT
Address: Pl. del Rei 11 (08002)
Telephone: 315 11 11
Metro: L4 Jaume I
Open: 9 am-8 pm, Tues-Sat; 3.30-8 pm, Mon.

The old Casa Padellàs dating from the 14th century; in 1962 declared an Historic-Artistic Monument; restored 1984-88 by Josep Maria Botey; the construction shows typical general layout of a nobleman's house of the Catalan-Gothic period decorated with surprising ornamental touches; entrance to the library executed by Josep Llinàs in 1990.

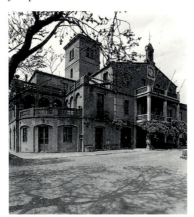

MUSEU VERDAGUER
Address: Vil.la Joana s/n (08017)
Telephone: 204 78 05
Metro: F.C. Catalunya, Vallvidrera
Open: 9 am-2 pm Tues-Sat.

Once an old country house known as Vil.la Joana, opened as a museum in 1962; the poet Mossen Cinto Verdaguer spent his last days here.

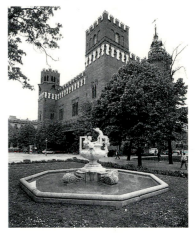

MUSEU DE ZOOLOGIA
Address: Pg. de Picasso 5 (08003)
Telephone: 319 69 12
Metro: L1 Arc de Triomf
Open: 9 am-2 pm, Tues-Sat.

Designed by Domènech i Montaner (1887-88), it was originally planned as a restaurant; incorporating neo-Gothic elements after Viollet-le-Duc, the building was known popularly as the 'Castle of the Three Dragons'; its unitary concept is of particular interest; remodelling carried out by Christian Cirici, Carles Bassó and Pep Bonet earned the FAD prize in 1988.

PIA ALMOINA
Address: Bisbe 5 (08002)
Telephone: 315 22 13
Metro: L4 Jaume I
Open: 10 am-1 pm, 5-8 pm, Tues-Sun.

After the collapse of part of the Canonja building in 1423, the Pia Almoina erected as centre for a charitable organization founded in 1009; restoration carried out by Josep Maria Botey in 1990, one of the pioneering activities in the creation of the Diocesan Museum of the Archdiocese of Barcelona.

MUSEU DE LA MUSICA
Address: Av. Diagonal 373 (08008)
Telephone: 416 11 57
Metro: L3 Diagonal
Open: 9 am-2 pm, Tues-Sun.

Known as the Palau Baró de Quadras and declared an Historic-Artistic Monument; building constructed by Puig i Cadafalch between 1904 and 1906; interiors maintain a certain level of diversity of design; since 1980 has housed the Music Museum.

MUSEU TEXTIL I DE LA INDUMENTÀRIA
Address: Montcada 12 (08003)
Telephone: 310 45 16 or 319 76 03
Metro: L4 Jaume I
Open: 9 am-2 pm, 4.30-7, Tues-Sat; 9 am-2 pm, Sun.

Originally of 14th-century construction, restored in 1969 for the installation of the Textile and Costume Museum; has Gothic and Renaissance elements due to various early alterations.

REIALS DRASSANES
Address: Pg. de Josep Carner 26 bis (08001)
Telephone: 301 18 71
Metro: L3 Drassanes
Open: 9 am-1 pm, 4-7 pm, Sat-Sun.

Shipyard's original construction dates from 1284-1348; has undergone different transformations and enlargements; latest restoration done by Adolf Florensa (1936-66); declared an Historic-Artistic

PRIVATE HOUSES

CASA BATLLÓ
Address: Pg. de Gràcia 43 (08007)
Telephone: 216 01 12
Metro: L3 Passeig de Gràcia
Open: 8 am-3 pm, Mon-Fri.

Built 1905-07 by Antoni Gaudí; in 1969 declared an Historic-Artistic Monument; Gaudí's original interior decoration is scrupulously preserved; note particularly the decoration on the main floor; in 1990 the ground floor restored as a commercial space by the architect Josep Maria Botey after being acquired by the company Iberia Seguros; interior by Nina Bernat i Elisabeth Vitri.

CASA MILÀ (LA PEDRERA)
Address: Pg. de Gràcia 92 (08008)
Telephone: 487 37 93
Metro: L3 Passeig de Gràcia
Open: 10 am-1 pm, Tues-Sat. Guided

tours available. Telephone for details.

Built 1905-10 by Antoni Gaudí; in 1969 declared an Historic-Artistic Monument; commonly known as 'La Pedrera', Gaudí built it while working on the Parc Güell and the Sagrada Família, immediately after finishing the Casa Batlló, with which there are certain resemblances; façade was constructed completely of stone, stonemasons made finishing touches on site.

EL CONVENTET
Now a private house and not open to the public; El Conventet became a part of the Santa Maria de Pedralbes Franciscan Monastery from the time of its foundation (1340) until the middle of the 19th century; for a time in the hands of the bishopric of Barcelona; at the beginning of the century, Enric Sagnier added a collection of 11th century Romanesque sculpture from Santa Maria de Besalú (Girona); in the 1940s, the architect Francesc Folguera and the decorator Jaume Llongueras renovated and enlarged the building, giving it a neo-Renaissance feeling.

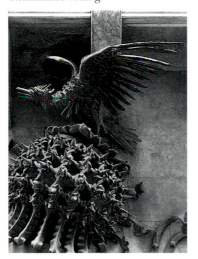

PALAU GÜELL
Address: Nou de la Rambla 3 (08001)
Metro: L3 Liceu
Not open to the public.

Built by Antoni Gaudí (1885-90) for the Counts of Güell; declared an Historic-Artistic Monument in 1969; one of Gaudí's most important works and the one which marks the beginning of the prime of his architectural work. Gaudí used the entire ornamental repertoire, interpreted by some as a precursor of *Modernisme*.

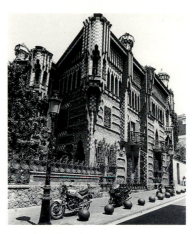

CASA VICENS
Private house not open to the public; designed in 1878 by Antoni Gaudí and constructed between 1883 and 1885, it was remodelled and enlarged by Joan B. Serra and was awarded the Barcelona Council Prize in 1927; in 1969 declared an Historic-Artistic Monument.

CASA BERENGUER
Address: Diputació 245 (08007)
Telephone: 301 00 30
Metro: L4 Passeig de Gràcia
Hall open: 8 am-10 pm. Visitors are generally not admitted to the other interiors.

Built 1907-08 by the brothers Joaquim and Bonaventura Bassegoda i Amigó; the high quality of the craftsmanship and profusion of decorative and sculpted elements combine to make it fine example of *Modernisme*.

CASA CALLEJO-AMAT
Private house not open to the public; house originally built as a summer home in 1929 after a French design, now used as a primary residence.

CASA LASALETA
Private house not open to the public; though the house itself is not especially interesting architecturally, Ignacio de Lasaleta who has lived here since 1979, has succeeded in creating a unique atmosphere.

CASA AMATLLER
Address: Pg. de Gràcia 41 (08007)
Metro: L3/L5 Passeig de Gràcia
Not open to the public

Built between 1898 and 1900 by Puig i Cadafalch, this house has a very peculiar style: a mixture of neo-Gothic, typical Netherlands and

Catalan architecture; of special interest is the finishing of the upper part of the façade which resembles houses in Bruges; at present houses the Amatller Hispanic Art Institute.

CASA SAYRACH
Address: Av. Diagonal 423-425 (08036)
Telephone: 202 06 86 (La Dama restaurant)
Metro: L3 Diagonal
Open: 1.30 pm-4.30 pm, 9 pm-11.30 pm, daily.

The municipal designs of 1915 are signed by Gabriel Borrell although their author was actually Manuel Sayrach; can be described as late *modernista* with Gaudian influences.

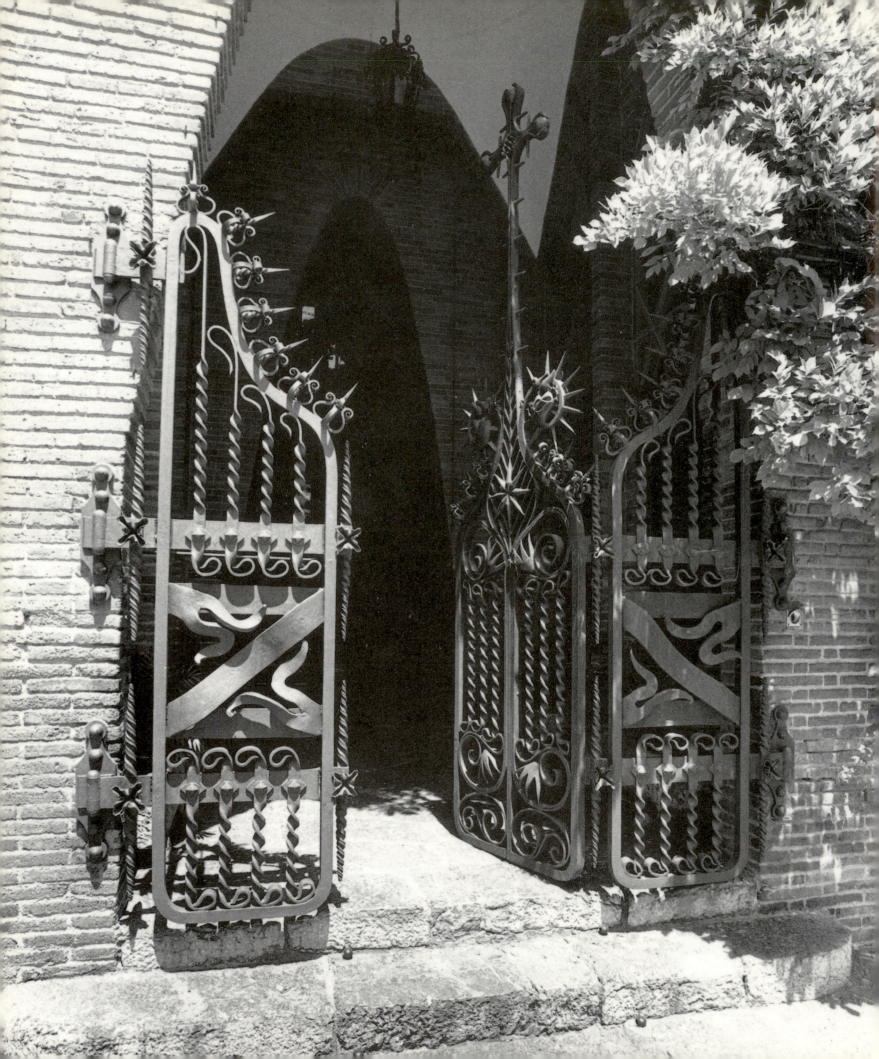

I N D E X

Page numbers in italics refer to illustrations

Aalto, Alvar, 24
Aigües de Barcelona, 47, *47,* 121
Ajuntament de Barcelona, 88, *89,* 123
Alarma i Moragas, Sàlvador, 120
Alberg Mare de Déu del Coll, 56, *56-7,* 121
Alfonso XIII, 17
Antonioni, Michelangelo, 13, 58
Arbei, Pere, 47, 120
Arnau, Eusebi, 55, 121
Arribas, Alfred, 69, 122
Art Nouveau, 10, 56
Arxiu Fotogràfic Mas, 71, *71,* 122
Aulenti, Gea, 124
Azulete restaurant, 63, *63,* 122

B.D. (Barcelona Design), 13, 120
Baldrich, Manuel, 121
Banca Catalana, 13, 44, *44, 45,* 120
Bassegoda, Joan, 122
Bassegoda i Amigó, Joaquim and Bonaventura, 125
Bassó, Carles, 124
Battló, Josep, 116
Beltxenca, 61, *61,* 122
Berenguer family, 116
Bertolucci, Barnardo, 64
Biblioteca de l'Ateneu, 74, *74,* 122
Biblioteca de Catalunya, 74, *75,* 122
Biblioteca del Collegi d'Advocata, 72, *72,* 122
Biblioteca de la Universitat, *70,* 71, 122
Blay, Pere, 122
Bofarull brothers, 66
Bona, Eusebi, 123
Bonet, Pep 124
Borrell, Gabriel, 110, 125
Bosch, Andreu, 124
Botey, Josep Maria, 124, 125
Brasserie Flo, 64, *64,* 121

Buñuel, Luis, 66
Busquets brothers, 31, 119

Caballé, Monserrat, 31
Café del Centre, 65, *65,* 122
Camiseria Xancó, 17, *17,* 119
Canyelles, Francesc, 51
Caracoles, Los, restaurant, 66, *67,* 122
Carbonell, Guillem, 87
Carlos III, 32
Carreras, José, 31
Carrió, Antoni, 123
Casa Amatller, 111, *111,* 125
Casa de l'Ardiaca, 73 *73,* 122
Casa Batlló, 7, 12, 115, 116, *116,* 125
Casa Beethoven, 22, *22,* 119
Casa Berenguer, 116, *116,* 125
Casa Callejo-Amat, 12, 109, *109,* 125
Casa Figueras, 18, 119
Casa Lasaleta, 125
Casa Lleó i Morera, 12, 44, *44,* 120
Casa Milà, 110, *110,* 115, 125
Casa Palau, 17, *17,* 119
Casa Sayrach, 110, *110,* 125
Casa Thomas (B.D. Edicions de Disseny), 24, *24,* 119
Casa Vicens, 112, *113,* 125
Catà, Enric, 124
Cendoya, Pedro, 124
Centre Cultural de la Fundació 'La Caixa', 13, *26,* 27, 119
Centre Excursionista de Catalunya, 27, *27,* 120
Cercle Eqüestre, 32, *32,* 119
Cercle del Liceu, 31, *31,* 119
Cerdà, Idelfons, 9, 11, 15
Cereria Subirà, 13, 20, *20,* 119
Cirici, Christian, 124
Civil War (1936-9), 10, 15, 56, 96, 121
Clínica Barraquer, 96, *96,* 124
Clotet i Ballús, Lluís, 124
Collegi d'Advocats, 28, *28,* 72, *72,* 119, 121
Collegi de les Teresianes, *50,* 51

Columbus, Christopher, 87, 101
Conselleria de Sanitat de la Generalitat de Catalunya, 96, *96,* 124
Conventet, El, *108,* 109, 125
Convention Bureau, 44, *44,* 120
COOB (Barcelona Olympics Organization Committee), 86
Coppola, Francis, 64
Cortés, Pepe, 122
Cuspinera, Lluís, 124

Dalí, Salvador, 17, 20, 83, 123
De los Angeles, Victoria, 71
Delegació del Govern a Catalunya, 90, *91,* 123
Dipòsit de les Aigües, 86, *86,* 124
Domènech i Estepà, Josep, 123
Domènech i Montaner, Lluís, 10, 24, 32, 44, 55, 95, 99, 119, 120, 121, 123, 124
Domènech i Roura, Pere, 124

Editorial Enciclopèdia Catalana, 32, *32,* 120
Eixample, 11, 13, 15, 24, 47, 52, 110, 116
Escola del Treball, 52, *53,* 121
Escola dels Jesuïtes de Sarrià, *48,* 49, 121
Escribà, Christian, 18, 119
Estació de França, *42,* 43, 121
Esteva, Joan, 119

Falguera i Sivilla, Antoni de, 123, 124
Falqués i Urpi, Pere, 93, 120, 124
Fargas, Josep Maria, 120
Farmàcia Mallol Balmaña, 18, *19,* 119
Felipe V, 15, 121
Fellini, Federico, 8
Fernández, Telm, 120
Fernando V of Castile, 9, 73, 87
Ferrer de Llupià, Josep Francesc, 122
Ferrés, Eduard, 121
Florensa, Adolf, 74, 122, 123, 125
Fochs, P., 120

Folguera, Francesc, 121, 125
Font, Josep, 122
Fontseré i Mestres, Josep, 86, 93, 124
Forestier, J. C. N., 85
Francesc de P. Nebot, Puig i, 123
Frare Blanc, El (El Asador de Aranda), *60,* 61, 121
Freixas, Jaume, 124
Freixes, Dani, 122
Fundació Joan Miró, 104, *104, 105,* 124

Galí, Francesc, 106, 124
Gargallo, Pablo, 35, 95
Garriga, Miquel, 120
Garriga i Molina, 32
Gaudí, Antoni, 7, 10, 24, 32, 51, 86, 110, 112, 115, 116, 121, 124, 125
Gelpí i Vintró, Lluís, 123
Genet, Jean, 11
Gil i Serra, Pau, 95
Goday i Casals, Josep, 51, 121, 124
Gonzàlez, Josep, 71, 122
Govern Civil, 12, 78, *78,* 123
Gran Teatre del Liceu, 31, 36, *36-7,* 120
Granell, Geroni, 44
Gris, Juan, 24
Gropius, Walter, 24
Grup Escolar Pere Vila, 51, *51,* 121
Guardia, Francesc, 119
Guastavina, Rafael, 52
Güell, Counts of, 115
Gustà, Jaume, 93

Hemingway, Ernest, 10
Herboristeria Enormes, 20, *21,* 119
Heron Building, 43, *43,* 120
Hervàs i Arezmendi, Joan Josep, 119
Hidroelèctrica de Catalunya, 93, *93,* 120
Homar, Gaspar, 44

INDEX

Hospital de la Santa Creu i Sant Pau, 95, *95*, 124
Hostalrich, Joan, 101
Hotel Comtes de Barcelona, 58, *58*, 121
Hotel España, *54*, 55, 121
Hotel Oriente, 58, *59*, 121
Hotel Ritz, 55, *55*, 121

Iberia Seguros, 125
International Exhibition (1929), 10, 15, 43, 106, 123
Isabel of Castile, 9, 87

Joanpera, Joan, 121
Joieria Roca, 23, *23*, 119
Jugendstil, 10
Jujol, Josep Manà, 122

Kraus, Otakar, 31

Lasaleta, Ignacio, 125
Le Corbusier, 24
Lió, Marquès de, 106
Llinàs, Josep, 124
Llobet, Pere, 123
Llongueras, Jaume, 125
Lloret i Homs, Joaquim, 124
Llotja de Mar, 13, *46*, 88, *88*, 120
Losey, Joseph, 13
Lozoya, Antonio, 120, 123

Madorell i Rius, Miquel, 120
Malraux, André, 10
Mandiargues, Pierre de, 11
Maragliano, Mario, 44
Maria de la Serra Godoy, Ignacio, 123
Maritime Museum, 11, 101
Marsans family, 56, 121
Marti, Antoni, 31, 119
Martorell, Joan, 121
Mas i Dordal, Josep and Pau, 123
Mas i Vila, Josep, 123
Mestre, Manuel, 120
Mestres, Josep Oriol, 120
Mies van der Rohe, Ludwig, 10

Miranda, Vicente, 122
Miró, Joan, 105, 124
Mitjans i Miró, F., 123
Modernisme, 10, 11, 15, 18, 27, 32, 44, 52, 61, 66, 90, 95, 96, 106, 111, 112, 119, 120, 121, 122, 123, 125
Molino, El, 40, *41*, 120
Montaner, Andreu, 43, 121
Montbui, Joana de, 101
Moragas i Gallissà, A. de, 8
Moragas i Spa, Antoni de, 121
Moses and Aaron (Schoenberg), 10
Moya, Joan, 123
Mudéjar style, 112
Muntanyà, Antoni, 121
Museu d'Art de Catalunya, 106, *106*, 124
Museu d'Història de la Ciutat, 101, *101*, 124
Museu de la Música, 102, *103*, 124
Museu Tèxtil i de la Indumentària, 106, *107*, 125
Museu Verdaguer, 99, *99*, 124
Museu de Zoologia, *98*, 99, 124

Network bar-restaurant, 69, *69*, 122
Nick Havanna, *62*, 63
Noucentisme, 15, 51, 121

Oliveras i Gensana, Camil, 96, 124
Olympic Games (1992), 11, 15, 86
Omnium Cultural, 29, *29*, *30*, 120
Orwell, George, 10

Palau Cassades, 28, *28*, 72
Palau Dalmases, 29, *29*
Palau Episcopal, 90, *90*, 123
Palau de la Generalitat de Catalunya, 12, 80, *81*, 122
Palau Güell, 115, *115*, 125
Palau de Justicia, *76*, 77, *77*, 123
Palau Macaya, 13, 27
Palau Moja, 79, *79*, 123

Palau Montaner, 90, *91*
Palau de la Música Catalana, 35, *35*, 64, 120
Palau de Pedralbes, 80, *80*, 123
Palau Reial Major, 87, *87*, 123
Palauet d'Albèniz, 83, *87*, 123
Paloma, La, dance-hall, 38, *38-9*, 120
Paricio i Ansuastegui, Ignacio, 122, 124
Parlament de Catalunya, *84*, 85, 123
Pastisseria Escribá, 18, *18*, 119
Pei, Josep, 44
Perales, Francesc, 71, 122
Pere III, 87, 101
Pia Almoina, 12, 102, *102*, 124
Picasso, Pablo, 66
Picasso Museum, 12
Pla, Francesc ('El Vigatà'), 79, 90, 122, 123
Pla, Josep 11
Puig i Cadafalch, Josep, 10, 27, 66, 102, 106, 111, 119, 121, 125

Quatre Gats, Els, café, 66, *66*, 121

Reial Academia de Medicina i Cirurgia, 7, 32, *33*, 120
Reials Drassanes, *100*, 101, 125
Renaixença, 10, 15, 31, 119, 120
Reporter, The (film), 13, 58
Residencia Francesc Layret, 96, *97*, 124
Riera, Mireia, 120
Rigalt, Joan, 44
Rocamora family, 106
Rodríguez, Ventura, 7, 32, 120
Rogent, Elies, 52, 71, 121, 122
Roma (film), 8
Roncali, Count, 78, 123
Ros de Ramis, Joaquín, 123
Roviralta family, 61
Rubió i Bellvé, Joan, 52, 61, 121, 122

Sabassona, Baron de, 74

Safont, Marc, 122
Sagnier i Villavechia, Enric, 32, 77, 10, 123, 125
Saló Daurat de Llotja, 88, *88*
Samsó, Edward, 63, 69, 122
Sanz, J. M., 120
Sayrach, Manuel, 110, 125
Schoenberg, Arnold, 10
Serra, Joan B., 125
Serra i Fiter, Antoni, 44
Serra i Pujals, Antoni, 119
Sert, Josep Lluis, 23, 104, 105, 119, 124
Simon, Claude, 10
Soler, Joan, 120

Teatre Arnau, 40, *40*, 120
Teatre Tívoli, 35, *35*, 120
Tinell, 13
Torra, A., 120
Tous, Enric, 120
Tusquets, Oscar, 120, 122

Umbracle, *92*, 93, 124
Universal Exhibition (1888), 9, 99, 123
Universitat Central de Barcelona, 52, *52*, 121

Velòdrom bar, 64, *64*, 122
Verdaguer, Mossèn Cinto, 99, 124
Vidal, Francesc, 31, 119
'Vigata, El' (Fransec Pla), 79, 90, 122, 123
Vila i Codina, Pere, 121
Vilaseca, Josep, 121, 123
Vincon, 13, 24, *25-6*
Viollet-le-Duc, Eugène, 52, 121, 124
Virgili, Pere, 32

Zsa-Zsa bar, 68, *68*, 122